KEN LO's MEMORIES of CHINA COOKBOOK

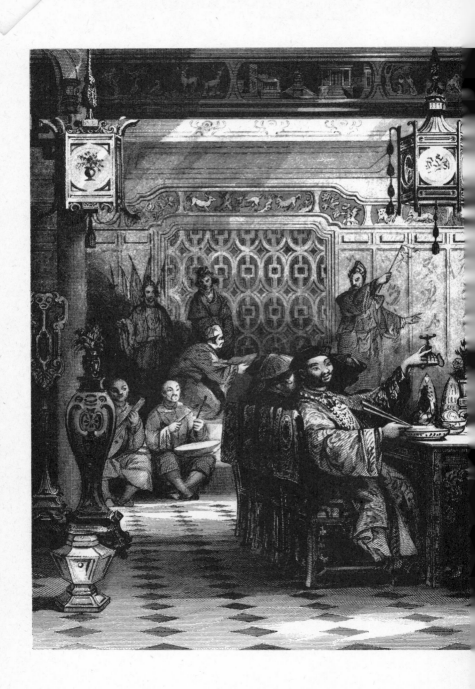

KEN LO's **MEMORIES** of **CHINA** COOKBOOK

Ken Lo and Kam-Po But

Whittet Books

First published 1982

Whittet Books, The Oil Mills, Weybridge, Surrey

Design by Richard Adams

British Library Cataloguing in Publication Data
Lo, Kenneth
  Memories of China cookbook.
  1. Cookery, Chinese
  I. Title II. But, Kam-Po
  641.5951   TX724.5.C5

ISBN 0-905483-22-7

Printed in Great Britain by the Pitman Press, Bath

Contents

Introduction

The 'Memories of China' was established as a restaurant in the summer of 1980 in one of the most exclusive districts of London. Ebury Street, where it is situated, adjoined the residences of Belgrave Square/Eaton Square, and the other smaller streets and squares which clustered around this fashionable area of the Victorian and Edwardian eras. Here lived the servants and tradesmen serving the grand houses. Even today there is a certain peculiar neighbourhood feeling (that cosy domestic 'upstairs downstairs' atmosphere) amongst the dwellers of this half square mile which gives them an entity that distinguishes them from all the other parts of the metropolis. What the 'Memories of China' has achieved in the very short time of its existence is to be able to blend itself into this unique background and atmosphere without feeling entirely extraneous, in spite of its having to draw its inspiration from and having its ultimate roots in Far Cathay.

During the little over a year of its existence, the Chinese food served at the 'Memories of China' has been recommended or acclaimed by international writers in, for example, the *New York Times,* the *Gourmet* Magazine of America, the *N.Y. Herald Tribune International, Figaro, L'Express, Feinsmecker* and *Gourmet* of Germany, the *South China Morning Post, Vogue, Harpers, House & Garden, Woman's Journal* and *Illustrated London News.*

What has enabled the food of the 'Memories of China' to make this unprecedented impact in such a short time? Apart from the high standard of cooking, this is due to the well selected grouping of dishes in its set menus, which give the diner a feeling of having gone through a memorable gastronomic experience at the end of a meal.

One of the main guiding principles in selecting our dishes is to achieve an amalgam of the characteristic flavours of the four main culinary regions of China — Peking, Szechuan, Shanghai and Canton (or respectively North China, West China, East China and South China), and to make them as authentic as we know how. This is not as tall an order as it may at first seem. On a recent gastronomic tour of China, I had the opportunity of visiting and eating extensively in all the four regions (and in Szechuan we even had the opportunity of attending a cookery school kitchen). Having savoured meals cooked in our restaurant kitchen (or cookery school kitchen) and those cooked and served in the different provincial corners of China, all within a very few days of one another, I have come to — I hope — the objective conclusion that the flavours and quality of foods cooked in such different circumstances and environmental backgrounds do not basically differ much. A 'Peking Duck' cooked in Belgravia is very much the same bird as a duck cooked in many restaurants in Peking, and frequently incontestably better! The same applies to many other dishes: notably the dish 'Squirrel Fish' which was very indifferent in the three different restaurants where we had it along the Lower Yangtze, in Nanking, Suchow and Yangchow. As for such Szechuan dishes such as 'Double Cooked Pork' 'Quick-Fried, "Yu Hsiang" Flavoured Shredded Pork', or 'Kung-Po Diced Chicken Cubes', since the flavours of such dishes are so pronounced — being hot and spicy — their characteristic flavour can be more easily reproduced than dishes of other regions of China which require more accurate tuning and representation, due to the finer nuances of flavours that need to be achieved. This is probably particularly true of the cooking and dishes of the East China region, of Shanghai and the Lower Yangtze. Because of the many prosperous towns and cities in this area along the river, such as Nanking, Suchow, Yangchow, in addition to Shanghai, we spent more days in this area during our gastronomic tour than anywhere else. In all I think we ate some nine or ten banquets in this region as well as many other types of daily meals. There seemed to be a predominance of fresh-water shrimps, crabs and lotus seeds, and a wide variety of vegetables in their dishes. Where these fresh-water foods required stronger flavouring, chopped-up salted pickles were often used to give them a spicier taste. There seemed a distinct reluctance to use heavy flavouring in stir-fry cooking, and as a whole there was a lighter touch as compared to what might be described as the coarser cooking of the North, which has a propensity to heavy use of garlic and soya paste. Because this Lower Yangtze is a very well watered region, there was a profusion of ducks on the table and these were often cooked long-steamed or long-braised as compared with the crispy skin variety of Peking (made crispy by roasting) or the Cantonese variety where the skin is made crispy more often by deep frying. When poultry and large chunks of meats are long-cooked they are often cooked to great tenderness, and are a boon to consume with rice. Rice is of course the principal crop of the region. Tou-Fu or bean curd also appeared on the table with frequency and in a variety of forms.

As a whole what the cuisine of this region seemed to emphasize was the richness and clear natural flavours of its products. As these attributes are less obvious than the overwhelming spiciness of the West, and the heavier flavouring of the North (of garlic, onion, sesame and soya), they are often more difficult to project in order to make an impact. Hence the comparative rarity of Shanghai and

Yangtze Chinese cooking abroad. Nevertheless this is a style of cuisine that possesses both considerable charm and appeal as well as a large repertoire of dishes, and an excellent contrast to the cooking of the other major regions.

Fortunately, two of the teachers in our cookery school, Mrs Fei and Mrs Liang, are native to this region. Hence they can hardly help but produce dishes which fall into the tradition in which they were born and bred. Mrs Liang's 'Shanghai Lion's Head Meat-Balls' and Mrs Fei's 'Crispy Skin Boneless Stuffed Duck' are among the finest dishes of their types I have ever tasted.

Therefore, by incorporating the talents and some dishes from our cookery school, we have no difficulty in providing and projecting an array of dishes which is truly representative of the characters and traditions of various regions of China. There is never any problem about finding Cantonese cuisine abroad, as over 80% of Chinese chefs working in the West are from Hong Kong and Kwangtung, the province in which Canton is situated, and they often know little else.

Cooking in a restaurant is always to a degree a manufacturing process (since many dishes are cooked dozens of times every day). The best establishments usually concentrate on the production of only a limited number of dishes in which they excel, rather than allowing the dishes to proliferate beyond reasonable control. The same applies to our kitchen. Any restaurant which is able to proffer a dozen or even half a dozen dishes of distinctive character and of the highest quality at a given time should be allowed to congratulate itself on having achieved remarkable results. This does not however mean that they do not possess another few dozen excellent dishes which are waiting in the wings, which can be rotated in the course of time, or called to the fore on special occasions.

This is exactly the situation with the 'Memories of China'. Although there are really no more than a dozen dishes or so that are distinctive to the restaurant, the whole menu, both 'à la carte' and 'table d'hôte', is constituted of over six dozen dishes. There are a further few dozen dishes, which can be 'tailor-made' or rather 'tailor-cooked' for special occasions; and still others which we would like to introduce or rotate onto the menu in due course.

In the catering situation of a restaurant, the measure of a dish depends not simply on its intrinsic excellence, but also on the facility with which it can be produced and incorporated into the production line. For when the evening's 'rush hour' arrives with the incoming tide of customers, some 200-300 well turned out dishes have to be cooked and served all within a couple of hours and there are no more than half a dozen chefs and cooks working over the cookers. Such work requires considerable discipline and expertise within the kitchen as well as understanding on the part of the management in feeding in the dishes ordered at a regulated pace, when the 'traffic situation' begins to border that of a rush-hour 'snarl up'; this happens almost every evening at any well patronized and popular Chinese restaurant.

It is precisely because of this situation that a great many dishes which we would otherwise dearly like to incorporate into the regular menu have had to be left out, or relegated into the category of 'banquet dishes', which are available only when ordered way ahead of time, so that they can be tailor-made for the occasion.

But in a recipe book we do not have to cope with the same difficulties. Here we enjoy far greater freedom. The problems of time and the process of production — or congestion of traffic — do not arise. Hence in compiling the recipes of this book we have been free to incorporate not only the dishes which are on our regular menu list of dishes, but also dishes which are not on the list, but which we should like to put on the menu and may do so in due course. In addition we have included a number of dishes which are being taught in several of the classes in our cookery school, and which we feel are intrinsically interesting. Thus between the covers of this book the reader will find not only more recipes than there are dishes on our restaurant menu, but also a more representative grouping of them from the different culinary regions of China.

The fun for the reader of this book is that, by trying out and experimenting with the recipes, he or she can in many cases also test their finished product against dishes that they can order on the floor of the restaurant, or seen demonstrated or tasted in the cookery school kitchen!

For the ease and convenience of locating dishes, the recipes which follow in this book are arranged in groupings which are normal on restaurant menus: namely under such categories as: 'starters', 'soups', 'principal dish', 'main courses' (those which are normally served with rice) or 'desserts'. Following these fairly long lists of dishes, we have also re-grouped some of the dishes into short menus, which are probably easier for readers to experiment upon if they are intent upon cooking Chinese for entertainment, whether domestically or socially.

There should be a sufficient number of recipes in the book to give you a taste of the essential flavours of China which are at the very heart of the Chinese way of life, and which have spanned the centuries. For those who are enthusiastic and stout-hearted enough to carry through experiments of cooking Chinese meals, I have no doubt that they will be rewarded by their own audacity and sense of exploration. For them, I wish loads of fun and many culinary discoveries and adventures!

The strength and appeal of the two set menus offered at the Memories of China is that having eaten the dishes, the consumer will have gone through a cameo of a gastronomic experience which is not easily forgotten. What perhaps creates most impact and imprints itself most indelibly on a person's palate is the conjunction of spicy dishes with those of light 'natural flavours' and the strong provincial characteristic of the dishes featured.

For our own historical record and the reader's interest I am reproducing these two menus below with a short 'commentary' to each dish in brackets:

MENU A
A 'Mini Banquet' : the 'Lobster Feast'

Starters:
   a)   Cantonese Ginger & Onion Lobster
      (a dish of matchless sea-savouriness)
   b)   Mongolian Barbecue of Lamb in Lettuce Puffs
      (a contrast of the meatiness of lamb with the fresh crispiness
      of lettuce laced with a piquant sauce)

Soup:
   c)   Peking Sliced Fish Pepper-Pot Soup
      (a warming soup of hot pepper impact)

Main Courses: Served with rice to 'cushion' the savouriness of saucey dishes
   d)   Szechuan Hot-Fried Crispy Shredded Beef
      (a distinctive spicy dish with sweet & sour appeal)
   e)   Shanghai Steamed Sea-Bass
      (sweet freshness of fish in ginger sauce)
   f)   Cantonese Quick-Fried 'three sea-flavours'
      (scallop, squid, and prawns in black bean sauce)
   g)   Quick-Fried Mange Tout
      (freshness and crispiness of fresh vegetables)

Dessert:
   h)   Ginger Ice-Cream with fresh fruit salad
     (a refreshing coolness which contrasts with all the preceding
     dishes)

MENU B
A Memorable Meal: the Duck & Prawn Dinner

Starters:
   a)   Cantonese 'Fresh Poached Prawns' with a piquant dip sauce
   b)   Peking 'Salt & Pepper Three Spiced Pork Choplettes'
      (hot spiciness of the dish imparts an arresting impact)

Soup:
   c)   Tou-Fu (bean curd), Prawns and Crab-Meat Soup

Principal Dish:
  d) Aromatic and Crispy Duck (the richness of the duck served rolled in a pancake is contrasted with the freshness of the shredded vegetables, and the sweet-sharpness of the 'Duck Sauce')

Main courses: Served with rice
  e) Iron-Plate Sizzled Chicken
      (a dish of natural flavour and light colour appeal)
  f) Cantonese Quick-Fried Sliced Beef in Black Bean Sauce
      (a spicy dish of warm earthy-savouriness)

Dessert:
  g) Fresh Sliced Chilled Oranges
      (what could be more refreshing after a hot savoury multi-course meal)

前菜

1. Starters

Sesame Prawn Toasts

(FOR 3-4 PEOPLE)

2 slices of white bread
2-3 oz. (55-85g.) sesame seeds
2 oz. (55g.) pork fat
4 oz. (115g.) shrimp or prawn meat
1 egg white
salt and pepper (to taste)
¼ tsp. MSG (monosodium glutamate) (optional)
3 tsp. cornflour oil for deep frying

Preparation
Chop pork fat and prawn meat very finely. Mix and blend well together. Add lightly beaten egg white, salt, pepper, MSG and cornflour and blend them well together. Spread the paste thickly on the 2 slices of bread. Spread sesame seeds evenly on a tray. Press the spread side of the bread slices on the sesame seeds to take on a thick layer.

Cooking
Heat oil until a crumb will sizzle when dropped into it. Lower bread, one slice at a time, into the hot oil face side (spread side) down to fry for 1½ minutes. Turn it over and allow it to fry for a further ⅔ minute. Remove the bread from the oil with a fish-slice. Allow it to drain for a short time on a piece of absorbent paper. Cut off the crusts from the edges.

Serving
Cut each slice of bread into 2 equal halves and further cut each half into 4-6 strip pieces. Serve hot and crispy.

Crispy Wontun with Sauce

Wontun skins are nowadays readily available from most Chinese supermarkets. The question now is simply one of wrapping a small amount of stuffing in the skins, and deep frying them for a matter of 2½-3 minutes until quite crispy. The wrapping of wontun is better seen than described: there are several ways of doing it, one of the commonest ways being to place about 1 tsp. of stuffing at the centre of the skin, and fold over from corner to corner, wetting a small part of the skin on the sides immediately around the stuffing and pressing them together.

Stuffings
Stuffing may consist of minced pork, often with chopped shrimps added. Use 1 tsp. stuffing per wontun; 3-4 wontuns per person.

Sauce
The sauce used is usually a 'sweet and sour sauce', which simply consists of mixing the following:

1 tbs. cornflour (blended in 4-5 tbs. water)
1 tbs. tomato purée
2 tbs. water
1½ tbs. orange juice
2½ tbs. vinegar
½ tbs. soya sauce
1½ tbs. sugar
½ tbs. vegetable oil

Put all the ingredients into a saucepan, and stir them together over medium heat for 3-4 minutes.

Crispy Seaweed

(FOR 4-5 PEOPLE)

2 lb. (1 kilo) selected spring greens (young cabbage)
2 oz. (55g.) split almonds
oil for deep frying
1½ tsp. caster sugar
1 tsp. salt
¼ tsp. MSG (optional)

Preparation
Cut out and discard the root of the cabbage; then slice cabbage with a razor-sharp knife into the thinnest possible shavings. Wash and dry thoroughly in a breezy spot either by spreading them out on absorbent paper or in a large wire colander (for about ½ hour). Deep fry or shallow fry the almonds until crispy.

Cooking
Heat the oil until it is about to smoke, and remove from the heat for ¼ minute. Add all the spring greens shavings. Stir and return pan to heat and fry for 2½-2¾ minutes. Remove and drain, then place on an absorbent paper to remove as much of the grease as possible.

Serving
Serve on a well heated serving dish, sprinkle evenly with sugar, salt and MSG, and add the fried almonds.

Peking 'Kuo Tieh' Steamed and Sauté Dumplings

(FOR 5-6 PEOPLE)

3 cups flour
⅔ cup boiling water
⅓ cup cold water
1 lb. (450g.) lean pork
4 oz. (115g.) shrimp meat
1 bunch watercress
1 tbs. chopped onion (or spring onion)
1 tbs. minced root ginger
1 tbs. light soya sauce
1½ tsp. salt
1 tsp. sugar
pinch each of pepper, MSG

Preparation
Add boiling water to flour in a basin. Mix and blend well by beating with a pair of chopsticks. Leave for a few minutes. Add cold water. Mix well and knead with hand.
    Chop pork and shrimp. Add chopped ginger and onion, salt, soya sauce, sugar and 1 tbs. water. Mix thoroughly. Chop watercress coarsely, add salt, pepper, MSG and 2 tsp. of oil. Mix and blend well. Add the watercress to the pork/shrimp mix. Beat them together

and blend well into a consistent paste.

Form the dough into a long 1¼" diameter stick. Break off at ¼" intervals, form into balls and roll flat into small pancake discs. Place 1 tbs. of pork/shrimp/watercress stuffing inside each pancake. Fold the pancake firmly in half over the stuffing and press and pinch the edges together to close.

Repeat until the materials are used up.

Cooking and serving
Heat a wok or frying-pan. When hot add 2-3 tbs. of oil. Tilt pan several times until its surface is evenly greased. Arrange the dumplings evenly over the pan. Turn the heat high to shallow fry for 2-3 minutes, which should brown the bottom of the dumplings. Add ⅔ cup of water. Place lid over pan. Continue to cook over high heat, under cover, until almost all the water has evaporated. Open lid, pour 1 tbs. hot oil in the sides. Lower heat, and cook until all the liquid has evaporated. Use a fish-slice to loosen the dumplings from the bottom of the pan. Turn a large serving dish face down over the dumplings in the pan.

Turn the pan and dumplings over so that the browned side of the dumplings will face upwards. Serve using soya sauce and vinegar as dips, or a mixture of the two.

Spring Rolls

(FOR 6-7 PEOPLE)

½ lb. (225g.) lean pork
5-6 Chinese dried mushrooms
2-3 oz. (55-85g.) bamboo shoots
½ lb. (225g.) young leeks
20 spring roll skins
1 tbs. flour
oil for deep frying

seasoning for the stuffings
½ tsp. salt
½ tbs. soya sauce
2 tbs. stock
1 tsp. sugar
2 tsp. cornflour (blended with 2 tbs. water)

Preparation and cooking
Cut pork into matchsticks. Soak mushrooms in warm water for ½

hour; then remove stems, and shred caps. Rub seasonings into the pork to season for ½ hour. Shred leeks and bamboo shoots.

Heat 3 tbs. oil in a frying pan. When hot add pork and stir fry for 2 minutes over high heat. Remove and put it aside. Add mushrooms and bamboo shoots to stir fry in the remainder of the oil for 2 minutes then remove and put aside. Add 1½ tbs. oil into the pan, and add the leeks. Stir fry the leeks for 1½ minutes. Return the previously stir fried pork, mushrooms and bamboo shoots to the pan. Add ¼ tsp. salt and 2 tbs. soya sauce, 1 tsp. sugar, 1 tbs. vegetable oil and 2 tbs. good stock. Stir fry over high heat until nearly dry. Pour in the blended cornflour evenly. Stir and turn for ½ minute. Remove the contents and place them in a bowl.

Wrapping
When somewhat cool wrap a suitable quantity of the stuffing in a sheet of spring roll skin in the form of a sausage roll, tucking in both ends and sticking the last flap or corner down with flour-paste. Repeat and arrange the spring rolls in a row with the flap sides down.

Frying
Heat oil in a deep fryer (or 1 pint oil in a deep frying pan). When a crumb will sizzle in the hot oil, lower the spring rolls (6 at a time) into the hot oil to fry for 2½-3 minutes. Remove and drain.

Serving
2-3 tbs. of soya sauce blended with 2 tsp. chilli sauce and 1 tsp. sesame oil can be recommended for use as a dip when serving and consuming spring rolls.

Quick-Fried Prawns on Sizzling Rice

(FOR 3-4 PEOPLE)

½-⅔ *lb. (225-290g.) fresh or frozen prawns*
1 egg white
1 tbs. cornflour
⅔ *tsp. salt*
oil for deep frying (¼ pint for shallow frying)
¼-½ *lb. (115-225g.) scrapings from bottom of rice cooker*

sauce

2-3 tbs. green peas
1 small can mushrooms (straw or button mushrooms)
¼ pint good stock
¼ tsp. MSG (optional)
½ tsp. salt
½ tsp. sugar
¾ tbs. cornflour (blended in 3 tbs. water)

Preparation
Thaw prawns and remove the shell and dark vein (if there is one).
Rub with salt, sprinkle and rub with cornflour, and wet with egg
white.
    Dry the rice scrapings by leaving them in an airy spot overnight
or longer; then put them in a pre-heated oven at low heat for ¼ hour.
Turn off the heat and leave rice to dry for a further 1 hour.

Cooking
Heat oil in a frying pan or deep fryer. When hot add the battered
prawns to fry for 1½ minutes and remove to drain.
    If a frying pan is used, pour away the oil (it can be re-used), add
the peas and mushrooms to stir fry in the remaining coating of oil
in the pan for 1½ minutes over medium heat. Add the stock, salt,
MSG (or 1 chicken stock cube, crumbled), sugar and bring to boil.
Add the blended cornflour. Stir quickly until the soup thickens.
Return the prawns to the soup, and bring to boil once more for ½
minute.

Serving
Place the hot rice scrapings in the bottom of a deep-sided serving
bowl or dish. Pour in all the contents from the pan over the hot rice,
which creates an explosive sizzle. The dish should be consumed as
soon as possible, before the crackling rice becomes soddened.

Cantonese Fresh Poached Prawns with piquant dip sauce

(FOR 4 PEOPLE)

1½ lb. (675g.) large shrimps (fresh or frozen)
4-5 slices root ginger
1 tbs. salt
3-3½ pints (2 litres) water

dip sauce
3 tbs. soya sauce
2 tbs. vinegar
2 tbs. shredded root ginger
3 tbs. stock
2 tbs. shredded spring onion
1 tbs. shredded chilli pepper
2 tbs. vegetable oil (very hot)
2 tsp. sesame oil

Preparation and cooking
Bring water to boil in a large pan of water with salt and sliced ginger. Clean shrimps and remove the heads. Pour the shrimps into the pan. When contents re-boil, simmer for 2 minutes and remove the shrimps to drain.

Prepare the dip by mixing the soya sauce with vinegar, stock, shredded ginger, onion and chilli. Boil oil in a small pan or metal ladle. When it smokes and is very hot, pour it in a thin stream over the dip ingredients which impregnates the sauce with flavour of the chilli, ginger and onion. Lace it with a few drops of sesame oil and the sauce is ready for use.

Serving and eating
The diner should peel the shell from the body of the shrimp and hold onto the tail to dip the flesh end of the shrimp into the dip sauce before eating.

Steamed Scallops in Black Bean Sauce

(FOR 4-5 PEOPLE)

10 large scallops (in shells)

For sauce
1 tbs. black beans
2 slices root ginger
2 spring onions
2 tbs. vegetable oil
1 tbs. light soya sauce
1½ tbs. dry sherry
1½ tsp. chilli sauce
3 tbs. good stock
1 tbs. vinegar

½ tbs. cornflour (blended in 2 tbs. water)
1 tsp. sesame oil

Preparation
Soak black beans in water for 20 minutes. Drain and chop finely.
Chop spring onions and ginger finely.

Cooking
Clean the scallops and place — still in their shells — on a dish or
tray and insert into a steamer; steam vigorously for 10-11 minutes.
   Heat oil in a small frying pan, and when hot add ginger, black
beans and onions and stir them around over medium heat for 1
minute. Add stock, soya sauce, chilli sauce and sherry. Stir them
together for a further 1¼-1½ minutes, or until the sauce has been
reduced to ½. Add vinegar, blended cornflour and sesame oil. Stir
and mix the ingredients together until well blended.

Serving
Apply 1-2 tsp. full of the hot blended 'sauce' to the scallop meat in
each of the shells and serve. An excellent and interesting dish for
a starter at a party dinner.

Crouton Studded 'Pomegranate' Crispy Prawn-Balls

(FOR 4-5 PEOPLE)

3-4 slices of white bread
½ lb. (225g.) filleted white fish
½ lb. (225g.) prawns (fresh or frozen)
2 tsp. salt
pepper (to taste)
2 slices root ginger
2 tbs. cornflour
2 egg whites
oil for deep frying

Preparation
Remove the crusts of the bread. Cut each slice into approximately
⅙"-⅐" crouton cubes. Place the croutons on a roasting pan and put
into a pre-heated low oven to dry and bake until slightly brown.
Spread them out on a large plate or tray. Chop fish and prawns
finely. Put them into a basin with salt, pepper (to taste), beaten egg

white, cornflour and finely chopped ginger. Mash until the mixture is well blended.

Form the fish prawn mixture into 1¾"-2" diameter balls, which should now be quite wet (because of egg whites) and the croutons should stick to them quite readily. Roll the 'prawn balls' over the spread-out croutons until they take on a coating or layer of them. Use loose croutons to cover the uncoated parts by sticking them on with fingers.

Cooking

Heat oil in the deep-fryer or 1 pint of oil in a frying pan until a crumb will sizzle when dropped into it. Add the crouton-studded prawn-balls into the hot oil one by one. Turn them around with a perforated spoon so that they are evenly fried. Remove them to drain after 2 minutes. One minute after all the prawn-balls have been removed and put aside, return them into the hot oil for a further ¾ minute deep frying.

Finally remove them all with perforated spoon to drain on absorbent paper.

Serving

A very useful dish to serve as a starter, using good quality soya sauce and ketchup with chilli sauce as dips, separately or mixed together.

Five-Spice Spare Ribs

(FOR 4-5 PEOPLE)

4-5 lb. (2-2½ kilos) spare ribs

dip sauce
4 tbs. soya sauce
2 tbs. vinegar
2 tbs. shredded root ginger
3 tbs. stock
2 tbs. shredded spring onion
1 tbs. shredded chilli pepper
2 tbs. vegetable oil (very hot)
2 tsp. sesame oil

Preparation

Use the same seasonings as in the preceding dip sauce recipe, and additionally sprinkle the spare ribs with 1 tsp. 'five-spice powder',

1 tbs. 'yellow bean sauce' (or 2 tbs. hoisin sauce) and 2 additional cups of stock, after having cut the meat into individual ribs.

Cooking
Cook all the ingredients together in a closed casserole for ¾-1 hour to tenderize the meat, as well as to reduce sauce to less than ⅓. In the process turn the ribs around 3-4 times. Leave the ribs in the sauce to further season until required.

Final cooking and serving
When required, place the ribs in a wire basket and deep fry for 4-5 minutes; then serve. Alternatively, place the ribs on a roasting pan, and insert them into a pre-heated oven at 200°C (gas mark 6; 400°F) for 10-12 minutes to crisp before serving. Heat the gravy at the bottom of the casserole; strain and pour it over the ribs as sauce.

Smoked Fish

(FOR 4-6 PEOPLE)

3 medium filleted plaice (or any flat fish)
1½ tsp. salt
1½ tbs. sugar
3-4 pieces of anise
4 tbs. soya sauce
2 tbs. dry sherry
½ cup good stock
¼ tsp. pepper
2 medium onions
3 slices root ginger
½ tsp. taste powder or MSG (optional)
3 tsp. sesame oil
oil for deep frying

Preparation
Cut onions into thin slices, shred ginger. Sprinkle and rub fish with salt and pepper. Place onions and anise in a flat-bottomed pan, add soya sauce, sugar, sherry, stock and taste powder. Mix well. Add the 3 pieces of plaice and bury them to season under the mixture for 2-2½ hours. Remove fish and put aside.

Cooking
Turn the heat on under the pan and cook briskly for 10-15 minutes. Add fish and turn it over 3 times in 15 minutes or until the liquid in

the pan has been reduced to less than $\frac{1}{4}$.

Leave the fish in the sauce to season further for another hour, without cooking. When required remove and deep fry the fish for $2\frac{1}{2}$ minutes. Remove and drain and sprinkle with sesame oil.

Serving
Cut the fish on a chopping board into $\frac{1}{2}''$ x 2'' pieces. It can be eaten hot or cold.

Deep Fried Crispy Giant Prawns in Breadcrumbs

(FOR 4-5 PEOPLE)

6-7 large Pacific prawns (fresh or frozen)
$1\frac{1}{2}$ tsp. salt
pepper (to taste)
$\frac{1}{4}$-$\frac{1}{2}$ tsp. taste powder (optional)
2 tbs. cornflour
1 egg white
$\frac{1}{4}$ lb. (115g.) breadcrumbs
oil for deep frying
3 tbs. soya sauce
1 tbs. chilli sauce

Preparation
Remove the shell (except tail), clean and cut each prawn into halves. Sprinkle and rub with salt, pepper and taste powder. Leave to season for $\frac{1}{2}$-1 hour.

Sprinkle and rub with cornflour and wet with egg white. Roll the prawns in breadcrumbs to take on a coating.

Cooking and serving
Heat oil in the deep-fryer until a crumb will sizzle when dropped into it. Put all the breadcrumbed prawns into the oil to deep fry for 2 minutes. Remove to drain on absorbent paper. Slice each prawn lengthwise into 2-3 strips. Serve to be eaten hot, using a mixture of 3 tbs. soya sauce with 1 tbs. chilli sauce as dip.

Peking Onion Pancake

(FOR 6 PEOPLE)

3 cups plain flour
1 cup boiling water
$\frac{1}{3}$ cup cold water
5-6 tbs. chopped onion (coarsely chopped)
3 tsp. salt
4-5 tbs. lard
4-5 tbs. vegetable oil

Preparation
Place flour in a basin. Pour boiling water into the flour in a thin stream, stirring and mixing all the time. Stir and mix until consistent. Wait for 3 minutes. Add cold water, mix and knead into a dough.
   Cover it with damp cloth and leave to stand for 20 minutes. Now divide the dough into 6 pieces and roll into 6 large pancakes (about 10-inch diameter). Sprinkle each pancake evenly with about 1 tbs. of coarsely chopped onion and $\frac{1}{2}$ tsp. salt. After spreading with $\frac{3}{4}$ tbs. lard, roll the pancake into a long roll. Press and close the 2 ends of the roll. Make the roll into a round flat spiral, and press flat with palm and roll with roller into a $\frac{1}{4}$ inch thick pancake.

Cooking
Heat oil in a large flat frying pan. Tilt the pan until the bottom is evenly greased. Spread the pancakes evenly over the bottom of the pan. Fry the pancakes as you would fry bread (only with less oil) over low-medium heat for 3 minutes. Turn them over and fry them on the opposite side for a further 2 minutes. The pan should be frequently shaken during the frying of the pancakes, which will help to prevent them from sticking.

Serving
Onion pancakes can be eaten on their own, or in conjunction with any savoury dish.

Radish and Spinach Salad

(FOR 4-6 PEOPLE)

12 selected bright red, medium sized radishes
$\frac{1}{2}$ tbs. salt
$1\frac{1}{4}$ lb. (565g.) young spinach

seasonings
1 tsp. salt
2-3 tsp. caster sugar
1/4 tsp. pepper
1/2 tsp. taste powder (MSG) (optional)
1 1/2 tbs. vegetable oil
2 tsp. sesame oil

Preparation
Cut away the roots of the radishes. Wash thoroughly and give each one of them a bash with the side of a heavy chopper to flatten them slightly. Sprinkle evenly with salt and leave to season for 1/2-1 hour.

Cooking
Poach the spinach (after removing any root or tough stems) in boiling water for 1/2 minute, and drain thoroughly. Chop the vegetable coarsely. Sprinkle evenly with salt, sugar, pepper, taste powder, oil and sesame oil.

Serving
Rinse radishes quickly under running water and dry with absorbent paper. Spread the spinach out evenly on a serving dish, and arrange the radishes on top.

Peking Salt and Pepper Three-Spiced Pork Chops

(FOR 4-5 PEOPLE)

1 1/2 lb. (675g.) pork chops
1 tbs. curry powder
3 eggs
5 tbs. cornflour
1/4 tsp. salt
1 tbs. water
oil for deep frying

for tossing in (before serving)
2 spring onions
2 tsp. ginger (powder) or 1 1/2 tbs. chopped root ginger
2 cloves garlic
1-2 green chilli pepper
salt and pepper (to taste)

Preparation
Chop pork chops into 1½"-2" size pieces. Sprinkle and rub with curry powder. Beat eggs and mix with salt, cornflour and water into a batter. Put the chops into the batter and coat evenly. Leave to season for a while.

Cooking
When the miniature pork chops have been seasoned, deep fry them in three batches for 7-8 minutes each (in not too hot oil) and drain.

Second stage (seasoning and serving)
Chop the spring onions, garlic, chilli pepper and ginger coarsely. Stir fry them in 1-2 tbs. oil for ½ minute. Add salt and pepper (to taste: about 2 tsp. salt and ½ tsp. pepper). Stir and turn the ingredients together a few times. Pour in the miniature pork chops and turn and stir them together to mix thoroughly and take on a coating of seasoning, then serve immediately.

Salt and Pepper 'Three-Spiced Hot-Fried Crispy Chicken'

Repeat the previous recipe substituting ½ medium chicken (about 3½ lb./1½ kilos) for pork chops.

Preparation
Chop the chicken through bone into large bite-size pieces. Sprinkle and rub evenly with curry powder. Repeat the process of coating with batter as in previous recipe.

Cooking
Heat oil in a deep-fryer (or 1 pint oil in a deep frying pan). When hot add the chicken pieces and fry for 3-3½ minutes. Drain away the oil (it can be re-used) and remove the chicken from the pan. Sprinkle the pan evenly with salt and pepper, ginger, garlic and chilli as in the preceding recipe. Place it over the heat for ¼ minute. Return the chicken pieces to the pan to stir-fry and turn over high heat for ¾-1 minute to take on a coating of hot seasonings and serve.

'Snow-Flake Prawn-Balls'

(FOR 4-6 PEOPLE)

½ lb. (225g.) shrimp or prawn meat
2-3 slices white bread
3 oz. (85g.) white fish
½ tsp. salt
2-3 water chestnuts
1 slice root ginger
2½ tbs. cornflour
oil for deep frying
1 egg white

Preparation
Remove the rinds from the bread, and cut into ⅙″ cubes. Spread the 'croutons' out on a roasting pan or heatproof dish, and bake in low oven for 8-10 minutes and leave them in to dry for further 1½ hours.
   Chop shrimp, fish and ginger finely, and water chestnuts coarsely. Mix them together in a mixing bowl. Add salt, water, egg white and cornflour. Stir and mix thoroughly until consistent. Form the mixture into 12-15 regular 1½″ diameter balls. Spread the 'croutons' evenly on a tray. Roll the now somewhat sticky prawn-balls over them to take on a layer of 'croutons'. Press pieces of 'croutons' on surfaces of prawn-balls which are still not covered with them.

Cooking
Heat oil in deep fryer. When a crumb will sizzle add the crouton-encrusted prawn-balls to the oil, one at a time. Fry them for 2 minutes. Remove with perforated spoon, and allow them to drain for 1½ minutes. Return the prawn-balls into the hot oil to fry for a further minute. Remove and drain on absorbent paper.

Serving
Serve on well-heated serving dish; consume hot. Useful dips for use with these prawns are ketchup, or salt-pepper mix (preferably briefly heated).

湯類

2. Soups

Hot and Sour Soup

(FOR 4 PEOPLE)

2 pints (1½ litres) good stock
1½-2 cakes bean curd
4 medium Chinese mushrooms (soak to soften in warm water for
*   20 minutes)*
2-4 tbs. cooked chicken meat (breast, leg, or from any part of the
*   bird)*
2 oz. (55g.) bamboo shoots
2 tbs. green peas
1 tsp. salt
1 stock cube
2 eggs

for flavouring and thickening sauce
2½ tbs. vinegar
1½ tbs. dark soya sauce
¼ tsp. freshly ground pepper
3-4 tbs. cornflour (blended in twice the amount of water)

Preparation
Shred chicken meat, mushrooms (discard stems) and bamboo shoots. Mix the ingredients of sauce in a bowl. Cut bean curd into small sugar-lump-size pieces. Beat eggs lightly.

Cooking
Heat stock in a large saucepan. Add mushrooms, bean curd, chicken, bamboo shoots, peas, salt, and stock cube. Bring to boil, and allow contents to simmer together for 5-6 minutes. Pour in the mixed sauce, and stir for 2 minutes until the soup has thickened somewhat. Now add the beaten eggs very slowly in a thin stream along the prongs of a fork, trailing the stream evenly over the surface of the soup.

Serving
Serve in a large bowl or tureen, so that the diners can help

themselves in the centre of the table, or divide the soup into individual bowls and serve in the western way.

Wontun Soup (with Chinese cabbage and mushrooms)

(FOR 4-6 PEOPLE)

20 wontun skins (available from most Chinese food-stores)
3-4 oz. (85-115g.) minced pork
2 oz. (55g.) minced shrimps
1-2 spring onions
salt and pepper (to taste)
1 tbs. cornflour
1 egg
2 pints (1½ litres) good stock
¼ lb. (115g.) Chinese cabbage
1 tsp. sesame oil
4-5 medium Chinese dried mushrooms

Preparation
Cut spring onions into small pieces. Soak mushrooms for 20 minutes in warm water, remove and discard stems and cut into quarters. Cut cabbage into thin slices. Put half the egg into a bowl containing minced pork, shrimps, spring onions and cornflour. Mix and blend well (with salt and pepper) until consistent. Stuff each skin with 1 tsp. of the above. Wet and seal with a small amount of leftover egg.

Cooking and serving
Heat stock until it boils, add the wontuns and mushrooms. When contents re-boil add cabbage and simmer for 10 minutes. Adjust for seasonings. Sprinkle with sesame oil and serve.

Tomato Soup with Bacon, Scallops and Shrimps

(FOR 3-4 PEOPLE)

1½ pints (1 litre) good stock
1½ tsp. salt
pepper (to taste)
1 chicken stock cube
2-3 slices root ginger
4-5 medium tomatoes
5-6 tbs. tomato purée
2 tbs. cornflour (blended in twice the amount of water)
4-5 tbs. shelled shrimps (fresh or frozen)
1½ rashers bacon
3-4 scallops
1 tsp. sesame oil
1½ tbs. dry sherry

Preparation
Chop ginger into fine pieces. Skin tomatoes and cut each into a dozen pieces, each scallop into quarters, and shrimp in halves. Cut bacon into small strips.

Cooking
Bring stock to boil. Add ginger, bacon and tomato, cook gently for 10 minutes. Add stock cube, tomato purée, salt and pepper and stir in the blended cornflour. Stir and turn until the soup thickens and is well blended.

Add the shrimps and scallops and allow the contents to simmer together for 3-4 minutes. Sprinkle with sherry and sesame oil and serve.

The Duck Carcass Soup

(FOR 5-6 PEOPLE)

1 duck carcass (left over after the bulk of the meat of the duck has been carved away to be eaten as 'Peking duck')
2½-3 pints bone stock
3 slices root ginger
2 tsp. salt
pepper (to taste)

1 chicken stock cube
½-¾ lb. (225-340g.) Chinese cabbage
1½ tbs. light soya sauce
2 stalks of young leeks

Preparation and cooking
Chop duck carcass into quarters or 6-8 pieces. Place them in a saucepan with stock. Bring to boil, add ginger and allow the contents to simmer gently for ½ hour. Add salt, pepper, soya sauce, stock cube.

Cut cabbage into 1½″ slices. Cut leeks into 1½″ sections after cleaning thoroughly. Add them all to the saucepan with the duck carcass and simmer gently for 15 minutes.

Serving
Serve either in a large soup tureen or casserole in the centre of the dining table to allow the diners to serve themselves by using a large ladle or soup spoon to transfer the required quantity of soup, cabbage and leeks into their own individual bowls (often their own rice-bowl).

The simple soup often proves very refreshing after a heavy savoury meal.

Sweet Corn, Prawn and Crab-Meat Soup

(FOR 3-4 PEOPLE)

1½ pints (1 litre) good stock
1-2 slices root ginger
1½ tsp. salt
¼ tsp. taste powder or MSG (optional) or 1 chicken stock cube
3-4 large shrimps or prawns
4-5 tbs. crab-meat
1 tbs. spring onions (freshly chopped)
1 8 oz. can ground sweet corn
1½ tbs. cornflour
1 tsp. sesame oil

Preparation
Blend cornflour in 3-4 tbs. water. Chop ginger finely. Cut prawns into thin slices.

Cooking

Heat stock in saucepan. Add salt, ginger and taste powder or stock cube. Bring contents to boil. Add crab-meat and sweet corn. Mix them well together, bring them to boil gently and simmer for 3-4 minutes. Add the remainder of the ingredients: blended cornflour, sliced prawns, spring onions and sesame oil. Mix and turn them over a few times and the soup is ready to serve.

Bean Curd, Prawns and Crab-Meat Soup

Repeat the above recipe, and add 1½ cakes of bean curd, cut into small sugar-lump-size pieces, in place of sweet corn.

Peking Sliced Fish Pepper-Pot Soup

(FOR 4 PEOPLE)

1½ pints (1 litre) good stock
1-2 slices root ginger
1 clove garlic
1½ tsp. salt
¼ tsp. MSG (optional) or chicken stock cube
½ tsp. freshly ground pepper
¼-½ lb. (115-225g.) filleted white fish (1 tbs. cornflour, 1 egg white,
½ tsp. salt)
2 tbs. wine vinegar
2 spring onions
oil for deep frying

Preparation

Cut fish into 1½" x 1" thin slices. Dust with salt and cornflour and wet with egg white. Immerse in hot oil to deep fry lightly for 1 minute and drain.

Chop ginger and garlic finely. Chop spring onions coarsely.

Cooking

Heat stock in a saucepan. Add ginger, garlic, salt, MSG or stock cube. Bring contents to boil and simmer gently for 1 minute. Add fish, vinegar and pepper. Simmer them together for 3-4 minutes. Sprinkle the top of the soup with chopped spring onions and serve.

Chicken and Asparagus Soup with Straw-Mushrooms

(FOR 4 PEOPLE)

1½-2 pints (1 litre) good stock
2-3 slices root ginger
1 tsp. salt
¼ tsp. MSG or 1 chicken stock cube
4-6 sticks of asparagus
1 small can straw-mushrooms
4-5 oz. (115-140g.) chicken breast meat
1 tbs. cornflour
1 egg white
1 tsp. sesame oil
oil for deep frying (or shallow frying)

Preparation
Cut chicken meat into 1½″ x 1″ thin slices. Dust with cornflour and wet with egg white. Deep fry them lightly in hot oil for 1 minute and drain. Remove the 1″ of the tough end of asparagus, and cut the remainder slantwise into 1½″ sections. Parboil them for 10 minutes in boiling water, and drain.

Cooking
Bring stock to boil in a saucepan. Add salt, ginger, MSG or chicken stock cube and asparagus. Bring to boil and simmer for 5 minutes. Remove ginger, add mushrooms and continue to simmer for 3-4 minutes. Add chicken and simmer for a further 2-3 minutes. Sprinkle the top of soup with sesame oil and serve.

Egg-Flower and Watercress Soup

(FOR 4-5 PEOPLE)

1½-2 pints (1 litre) good stock
2 slices root ginger

1 clove garlic
1 chicken stock cube
2 spring onions
½ bundle watercress
1 egg
1 tsp. salt
¼ tsp. pepper
1 tsp. sesame oil

Preparation
Chop garlic and ginger finely and spring onions coarsely. Remove the root of watercress and cut the bundle through 5-6 times after washing thoroughly.
   Beat egg lightly with a fork for ½ minute, then sprinkle with a pinch of salt and pepper.

Cooking
Heat stock in a saucepan. Add garlic, ginger, stock cube and watercress. Bring contents to boil and simmer for 3 minutes. Pour the beaten egg in a very thin stream, along the prongs of a fork, and trail it over the surface of the soup. When the egg has set, sprinkle the soup with chopped spring onions and sesame oil, and serve.
   (Although the soup is simple, it is an extremely popular and effective soup, frequently served in China.)

Spare Rib Soup with Chinese Cabbage or Broccoli

(FOR 4 PEOPLE)

1½-2 pints (1 litre) good stock
1 lb. (450g.) spare ribs
2-3 slices root ginger
1 clove garlic
1½ tsp. salt
1 chicken stock cube
pepper (to taste)
½ lb. (225g.) Chinese cabbage (or broccoli)

Preparation
Chop spare ribs through bone into 1½" sections. Parboil in 2 pints (1½ litres) boiling water for 5 minutes. Skim off the scum and pour away about ⅔ of the water. Allow the ribs to simmer gently for the

next hour. Crush garlic finely. Cut cabbage (or broccoli) into 1½"
pieces.

Cooking
Put root ginger, garlic and stock into the pan containing the ribs.
Bring contents to boil. Add salt, stock cube, pepper and cabbage (or
broccoli). Bring contents to boil once more and simmer gently for
the next 15 minutes.

Serving
Remove the ginger and serve by dividing the contents equally
between 4 soup bowls. The meat on the ribs can best be eaten by
first dipping the individual pieces of ribs in soya sauce, or soya
sauce reinforced with a small amount of chilli sauce.

White Fish Soup with Sizzling Croutons

(FOR 4 PEOPLE)

1½ pints (1 litre) good stock
1 tsp. salt
¼ tsp. white pepper
1 chicken stock cube
3 slices root ginger
½ lb. (225g.) filleted white fish
1 egg white
2½ tbs. cornflour
½ tsp. salt
1 slice white bread
1½ tbs. minced cooked ham
oil for deep frying

Preparation
Chop fish very finely. Add salt, egg white and cornflour and
beat them together with 5-6 tbs. water until consistent. Cut bread
into half-sugar-lump-size croutons.

Cooking
Heat stock in a saucepan. Add salt, pepper, stock cube and ginger.
Bring contents to boil and simmer for 3 minutes and remove ginger
with perforated spoon. Stir the beaten fish/egg white/cornflour
mixture into the soup slowly, stirring and mixing all the time.

When contents boil reduce heat to low and allow contents to continue to simmer gently.

Meanwhile heat oil in pan or deep-fryer until very hot. Add the croutons to deep fry until nearly brown. Remove and drain with perforated spoon and transfer into the bottom of a very well heated soup bowl or casserole. Bring the latter to the table and pour in the fish soup, which should create an audible sizzle. Sprinkle with minced ham and serve.

Peking Sliced Lamb and Cucumber Soup

(FOR 4-5 PEOPLE)

½ lb. (225g.) leg of lamb
⅚" section of cucumber
2 pints (1½ litres) chicken stock
salt and pepper
1¼ tbs. vinegar
1 tbs. soya sauce
1½ tsp. sesame oil
1 chicken stock cube (crumbled)

Preparation
Cut lamb with sharp knife into 1½" x 1" very thin slices. Sprinkle and rub with soya sauce and sesame oil. Leave to marinate for 10-15 minutes. Cut cucumber into similar thin slices.

Cooking
Heat stock in a saucepan. Add salt, pepper (to taste) and stock cube. Bring to boil. Add sliced lamb to poach in the stock for 1 minute and remove. Add cucumber and bring to boil once more. Reduce heat and simmer for 2 minutes.

Serving
Just before serving add vinegar and return the lamb to the pan. Bring contents to boil once more, and serve.

Tou-Fu, Bean Curd and Spinach Soup

(FOR 3-4 PEOPLE)

1 small carton of frozen spinach
1 cake of bean curd
3-4 Chinese dried mushrooms
3-4 oz. (85-115g.) lean pork
1-2 slices of ham
1½ pints (1 litre) good stock
2 tsp. salt, pepper
2-3 tbs. cornflour

Preparation
Thaw the spinach and chop coarsely. Cut bean curd into small sugar-lump-sized pieces. Cut pork into ½″ slices. Soak mushrooms in warm water for 15 minutes, discard stems, and shred caps. Chop ham into small pieces.
   Mix cornflour with three times its volume of water, until well blended.

Cooking
Bring stock to boil in a saucepan. First add pork, ham, mushrooms and bean curd. When they have boiled for five minutes stir in the spinach, followed by blended cornflour to thicken the soup, turn off the heat and sprinkle the soup with pepper (to taste).

Serving
Serve in large soup bowl or casserole for diners to help themselves, or divide into individual soup bowls.

Shark's Fin Soup

(FOR 4-5 PEOPLE)

3-4 oz. (85-115g.) shark's fin
3-4 slices root ginger
6-8 medium Chinese dried mushrooms
4-6 oz. (115-170g.) chicken breast meat (fresh)
3-5 oz. (85-140g.) crab-meat
1½-2 pints (approx. 1 litre) finest stock
1 tsp. salt
¾ tbs. dark soya sauce

pinch of pepper
½ tsp. MSG (optional)
2½ tbs. cornflour (blended in 4-5 tbs. water)
½ tsp. sesame oil

Preparation

Soak shark's fin overnight. Drain and simmer shark's fin in 2 pints water for 1½ hours with ginger. Drain and simmer again in 1 pint stock for ¾ hour, remove and drain.

Soak mushrooms in water for ½ hour and drain. Remove stems and cut caps into quarters.

Cooking and serving

Heat stock in an enamel or ceramic pot. When hot add mushrooms and shark's fin and simmer for 15 minutes. Add salt, pepper, soya sauce, MSG and crab-meat and bring to rolling boil for a few minutes. Add chicken (fresh shredded) and cornflour mixture. Stir and cook for 3-4 minutes. Sprinkle with sesame oil and serve.

雞鴨

3. Poultry

Quick-Fried Diced Chicken Cubes with Walnuts

(FOR 5-6 PEOPLE)

1 lb. (450g.) breast of chicken
1 green pepper
1 red pepper
3 spring onions
2-3 slices root ginger
1 cup walnuts
4 tbs. sherry
oil for shallow frying (¼ pint; 145 ml.)

to add to chicken
½ egg white
1 tbs. soya sauce
1 tbs. cornflour

for sauce (to be blended together)
2 tbs. soya sauce
2 tsp. vinegar
1 tbs. dry sherry
1 tsp. cornflour
½ tsp. salt
2 tsp. sugar

Preparation
Cut chicken into pieces the same size as walnuts. Add a mixture of the egg white, cornflour and soya sauce to marinate for ½ hour. Cut pepper into ¾″ pieces, and spring onions into 1½″ sections.

Cooking and serving
Heat wok or pan. Add oil for shallow frying. When hot add the walnuts and stir fry over medium heat for about 3 minutes. Remove and drain on absorbent paper. Pour away most of oil from pan, retaining only 3-4 tbs.
Replace pan over medium heat. When hot add the chicken pieces

and stir fry for about 2½ minutes. Remove and drain.

Add 2 tbs. oil to the pan. Place it over high heat. Add ginger, spring onions and pepper. Stir fry quickly for ½ minute. Add the blended sauce mixture and sherry and stir half a dozen times with other contents of the pan. Finally return the chicken pieces to the pan, stir and toss together with the other ingredients for ½ minute still over high heat. Remove and transfer to the centre of a serving dish.

Return the pan over the heat. Add the walnuts. Stir them over medium heat for ½-¾ minute. Remove and arrange them around the chicken/pepper on the serving dish and serve.

Iron-Plate Sizzled Chicken

(FOR 4-5 PEOPLE)

½ lb. breast of chicken
1 egg white
1 tbs. cornflour
1 tsp. salt
¼ tsp. MSG (optional)
2-3 stalks of green celery
pepper (to taste)
2-3 tbs. vegetable oil
2 slices root ginger
vegetable oil for deep frying
5 tbs. good stock
½ tbs. cornflour (blended in 3 tbs. water)

Preparation
Cut chicken into 2" x 1½" thin slices. Sprinkle and rub with salt, pepper and MSG, and wet with egg white. Cut celery slantwise into 2" sections.

Cooking
Heat oil in the deep fryer, or ½ pint oil in a frying pan. When hot add the chicken pieces, turn them over a few times, and remove pan from heat. Turn the chicken pieces over a few more times. Remove them from the pan to drain.

Meanwhile pour away the oil from the pan (if a frying pan is used), and add the celery and ginger to the pan. Stir them over high heat in the remaining oil for 1½ minutes. Add the stock. On boiling stir in the blended cornflour. Stir quickly until the sauce thickens. Return the chicken pieces to the pan to stir with the sauce and the celery for ½ minute. Pour the contents from the pan into a deep-sided bowl.

Serving

Heat the iron-plate over the cooker until nearly red hot. Bring it to the table, and pour the chicken, celery and sauce into the iron-plate, which creates an explosive sizzle. The diners should enjoy both the contents of the dish, and the drama.

Plain Long-Simmered Duck (or chicken) with Chinese Cabbage

(FOR 5-6 PEOPLE)

1 medium (3-4 lb./1½-2 kilo) duck
1 piece bacon bone (about 1½-2 lb./¾-1 kilo)
3-4 slices root ginger
3 tsp. salt and pepper (to taste)
1 2½ lb. Chinese cabbage
2 chicken stock cubes

Preparation and cooking

After cleaning duck (remove the oil sac from tail end) put it and bacon bone with ginger into a large casserole of boiling water. Bring to boil for 7-8 minutes. Skim away the scum. Close the lid of the casserole and insert into pre-heated oven at gas mark 3-4 (about 180-190°C; 350-375°F) for 2 hours. Remove the bacon bone, and skim away any excess oil. Add stock cube and insert the cabbage (cut into 2″ sections) around and under the duck. Return the casserole to the oven to cook for another ½ hour.

Serving

Serve straight from the casserole. The duck meat should be tender enough to take to pieces with a pair of chopsticks. It is best eaten dipped in thick soya sauce, or soya sauce mixed with chilli sauce.
   The cabbage is enjoyable as an accompanying vegetable.

Szechuan Rice and Tea-Smoked Chicken

(FOR 6-8 PEOPLE)

1 medium chicken
2 tsp. salt
2 tbs. soya sauce
2 tbs. dry sherry
1½ tsp. black pepper
3 tsp. vegetable oil
3 tsp. sugar
½ tsp. taste powder (MSG) (optional)
4 slices root ginger
3 spring onions
3 pieces chilli pepper
3 pieces anise

for smoking
3 tbs. tea leaves
3 tbs. brown rice

for gravy
1 tbs. soya sauce
1 tbs. sherry
2 tbs. good stock
1 tsp. chopped onion
1 tsp. chopped ginger
1 tsp. chopped garlic
2 tsp. sesame oil

Preparation
Rub chicken inside and out with oil, salt, soya sauce, sherry, sugar, pepper and taste powder. Shred the ginger, spring onions and chilli pepper. Stuff some of the latter in the cavity of the bird, and place the rest on top. Add 3 pieces of anise into the cavity of the chicken. Wrap the chicken up securely in tinfoil.

Cooking
Put the tinfoil-wrapped chicken in a steamer to steam for 1¾ hour. Then remove the tinfoil and place the chicken in a heatproof bowl and steam for a further ½ hour. Retain the liquid in the bowl for use as gravy.

Smoking
Mix the tea with brown rice, and place them at the bottom of a large

saucepan (reserved specially for smoking). Place chicken on top of a raised wire-frame, and lower the latter into the saucepan. Close the lid firmly. Place the saucepan over medium heat for 5 minutes, after which a considerable amount of smoke will have been generated. Turn heat off and leave the chicken to smoke in the enclosed pan for a further 5 minutes.

Serving
Transfer the smoked chicken to a heated serving dish. Reduce the sauce from the bowl in which the chicken was steamed by half, after adding 1 tbs. each of fresh soya sauce and sherry and 2 tbs. good stock, 1 tsp. each chopped onion, ginger and garlic and stirring over medium heat. Pour this gravy over the chicken, and sprinkle with 2 tsp. sesame oil, and serve. Alternatively the chicken can be chopped into 16-20 bite-size pieces first, with 'gravy' poured over them and served.

Szechuan Rice and Tea-Smoked Duck

Repeat the previous recipe, substituting duck for chicken.

Peking Kuo Ta Sautéed Sliced Chicken

(FOR 4-5 PEOPLE)

8 oz. (225g.) large slices of breast of chicken
4 eggs
3 slices ginger
4 cloves garlic
4 spring onions
6 tbs. vegetable oil
8 tbs. good stock
½ tsp. flavour powder (MSG) or 1 crumbled chicken stock cube
1 tbs. light soya sauce
1 tsp. salt
pepper (to taste)
2 tbs. dry sherry

Preparation
Season chicken with salt and pepper. Beat egg lightly, and add the slices of chicken. Chop 3 slices of ginger, 4 cloves of garlic and 4 stalks of spring onion coarsely. Combine stock with crumbled stock cube, soya sauce and sherry.

Cooking and serving
Heat oil in a wok or large frying pan. When hot add the pieces of egg-battered chicken slices, and lay them out evenly at the bottom of the pan. Sauté until the egg has set (and is about to turn brown). Sprinkle with half the chopped ginger and onions and turn them over to sauté for 1½ minutes. Pour in half the stock/soya/sherry mixture and cook for a further ½ minute. Lift the chicken slices out from the pan with a fish-slice. Place on a chopping board and cut into 1½″ wide slices and transfer to a well-heated serving dish. Meanwhile add remainder of the chopped ginger, garlic and onions to the pan, along with the rest of the soya stock sherry mixture. Boil fast and pour it evenly over the chicken slices in the serving dish as sauce.

Salt and Pepper 'Three-spiced Chicken'

(FOR 4-6 PEOPLE)

1 small chicken (2-3 lb./1-1½ kilos)
2½-3 tbs. curry powder
1 egg
2 tbs. water
2 tsp. cornflour
4 tbs. self-raising flour
3-4 chilli peppers
1½ tbs. sea salt
1 tbs. pepper corns
oil for deep frying

Preparation
Remove head and feet of chicken. Cut chicken through bone into about 20 pieces. Sprinkle and rub with curry powder. Mix and beat cornflour and self-raising flour in a basin with egg and water into a consistent batter. Add the pieces of chicken, turn them in the batter until they are evenly coated. Shred the chilli pepper and pound the pepper corns with side of chopper or in a mortar until crushed.

Cooking and serving
Heat oil in saucepan or wok until a crumb will sizzle audibly when dropped into it. Add the chicken pieces one by one, turn them around and allow them to fry for 3-3½ minutes. Remove them to drain.

Heat a wok or frying pan over medium heat and add 2 tbs. oil. When hot add chilli pepper, pepper corns and salt. Stir them around widely to cover evenly the bottom of the pan for 1½ minutes. Increase heat to high, and pour in the pieces of chicken. Stir and turn them around quickly for 2 minutes and serve — to be eaten hot.

Cantonese Hot-Fried Black Bean Chicken

(FOR 4-5 PEOPLE)

⅔ lb. (285g.) breast of chicken
2 tbs. cornflour
1 egg white
2 slices root ginger
4 tbs. vegetable oil
2 chilli peppers (fresh or dried)
1 sweet pepper (green or red)
1 tbs. salted black beans

Preparation
Cut chicken into sugar-lump-size cubes. Dust with cornflour and wet with egg white. Shred chilli pepper and cut sweet pepper into 1½″ x 1″ pieces, discarding pips. Soak black beans in water for 10 minutes and drain off water.

Cooking
Heat 3 tbs. oil with ginger in a frying pan or wok for ½ minute. Remove ginger. Add chicken pieces. Stir them over high heat for 2 minutes, and remove. Add remaining oil, black beans, chilli pepper and sweet pepper. Mix the black beans with the oil in the pan, and stir the pepper around for 1½ minutes. Finally return the chicken to the pan and continue to stir fry over high heat for 1½ minutes. Serve hot.

Peking Quick-Fried Diced Chicken in Soya Paste Sauce

(FOR 4 PEOPLE)

3/4 lb. (340g.) breast of chicken
1 egg white
2 tbs. cornflour
3 slices root ginger
4 tbs. vegetable oil

for sauce
2 tbs. yellow bean sauce
3 tsp. sugar
2 tsp. cornflour (mixed with 3 tsp. water)

Preparation
Cut chicken meat into sugar-lump-size cubes. Dust with cornflour and wet with egg white.

Cooking and serving
Heat 3 tbs. oil with ginger in frying pan or wok. When hot add the chicken cubes and stir fry for 1½ minutes. Remove the chicken cubes and ginger pieces and put aside.

Add remainder oil, yellow bean sauce and sugar. Mix them together over medium heat for ½ minute. Add the blended cornflour, and mix it with the yellow bean and sugar sauce, until the mixture is shiny and creamy.

Return the fried chicken cubes to the pan and stir together with the sauce until every piece of chicken cube is coated with it. Serve immediately.

Cantonese Steamed Chicken with Chinese Sausage and Black Mushrooms

(FOR 4-5 PEOPLE)

½ lb. (225g.) chicken breast meat
3 Chinese sausages
1 tbs. cornflour (mixed with 3 tbs. water)

9 large Chinese dried black mushrooms
½ lb. (225g.) broccoli
1½ tsp. salt
1¾ tbs. chopped onion
2½ tsp. chopped garlic
2 tsp. sugar
1 tbs. light soya
1½ tbs. dry sherry
1½ tbs. good stock
1 tbs. vegetable oil
2 tsp. sesame oil

Preparation
Rub chicken with salt and mix with half the onion and garlic. Leave to season for half an hour. Soak dried mushrooms also for ½ hour. Meanwhile mix the remaining half of onion, garlic and cornflour with sugar, soya, oil, sherry, stock and sesame oil. After dipping the mushrooms, broccoli, chicken and sausage in the mixture, arrange them, interleaved with one another, on a heatproof dish.

Cooking
Put the dish into a steamer, and steam vigorously for 8-10 minutes.

Serving
Bring the dish to the table in a cloud of steam, and serve directly from the steamer.

Long-Simmered Chicken with Chinese Cabbage

(FOR 7-8 PEOPLE)

This is an extremely simple dish, but adding a quantity of Chinese cabbage to the pot a quarter half an hour before the dish is ready for serving brings a sweetness into the dish which lifts it to the level of haute cuisine.

1 chicken (3-4 lb./1½-2 kilos)
2½ tsp. salt
4 slices root ginger
2 chicken stock cubes (or ½ tsp. MSG & 1 tsp. salt)
1½-2 lb. (¾-1 kilo) Chinese cabbage
2 pints (1½ litres) water

Preparation
Parboil the chicken in a large pan of boiling water for 5-6 minutes and drain. Remove the root of the cabbage, and cut the leaves slantwise into pieces 3″-4″ long.

Cooking
Place the chicken in a large casserole and add salt, ginger and 2 pints of water. Bring contents to boil, and put the casserole into a pre-heated oven at gas mark 3 (180°C; 350°F) to cook for 1½ hours. Turn the bird over every ½ hour. After 1½ hours, open the lid of the casserole, and lift up the chicken slightly; insert the cabbage and crumbled stock cubes underneath it and continue to cook for a further ½ hour.

Serving
When ready the casserole should be brought to the table. The chicken should be tender enough to take to pieces with a pair of chopsticks and is eaten dipped in soya-chilli dip. The cabbage should also be ladled into the diners' individual bowls.

Lotus-Leaf-Wrapped and Long-Steamed Stuffed Chicken

(FOR 5-6 PEOPLE)

1 chicken (about 4 lb./2 kilos)
2 large sheets of dried lotus leaves (available in many Chinese food-stores)
1 large sheet tinfoil
2 tbs. soya sauce
2 tbs. hoisin sauce

for stuffing
2½ cups glutinous rice
2 medium size onions
6 chestnuts
6 dried Chinese mushrooms
3-4 tbs. diced ham
2 tsp. salt
2 tbs. dried shrimps
3-4 tbs. diced bamboo shoots
3 slices root ginger
4 tbs. vegetable oil
3 cloves garlic

Preparation
Rub the chicken inside and out with an equal mixture of soya sauce and hoisin sauce and leave to season for ½ hour while you prepare the stuffings. Soak the lotus leaves in water for a couple of minutes to soften, and drain. Soak all the stuffing ingredients which require soaking for 20-30 minutes. Remove stalks from mushrooms and dice caps into ½" square pieces. Chop shrimps, garlic and ginger coarsely. Cook rice in water for 4-5 minutes and drain.

Cooking
Heat oil in a wok or large frying pan. Add ginger, onions, garlic and shrimps and stir fry together for 3-4 minutes. Add all the other ingredients, and continue to turn and stir fry for a further 3-4 minutes.

Rub the chicken once more with the remainder of the soya/hoisin sauce mixture before stuffing it with all the stuffing ingredients. Sew up the chicken so that stuffings will be secure.

Wrap the chicken with the 2 sheets of lotus leaf, and by way of making it secure, wrap the tinfoil over the lotus leaf bundle once or twice. Place the twice-wrapped chicken in a heatproof dish, and insert into a steamer; steam steadily for 2½-3 hours.

Serving
Bring the chicken to the table on a large plate. Unwrap the 2 layers of wrappings. The chicken should now be sufficiently tender to take to pieces with a pair of chopsticks. The stuffings can be ladled out into the individual bowls of the diners to be eaten with the chicken.

Lotus-Leaf-Wrapped Long-Steamed Duck

Repeat the preceding recipe, substituting duck for chicken.

The Szechuan Bang Bang Chicken

(FOR 8-10 PEOPLE)

1 large, or 2 small, chickens
1 medium cucumber

for sauce
4 tbs. peanut butter
2 tbs. sesame oil
1 tsp. sugar
½ tsp. salt
3 tbs. good stock
3 tsp. 'red oil'

Preparation and cooking
After cleaning the chicken or chickens thoroughly boil it in a large saucepan of water for ½ hour. Remove the chicken breasts, and cut them into triple-matchstick-sized strips. Clean cucumber and cut it into similar size strips as the chicken. Spread the cucumber as a bed on a large serving dish, and pile the shredded chicken evenly on top in a mound.

Preparing the sauces and serving
Mix the peanut butter with sesame oil, stock, sugar and salt in a bowl until well blended. Pour the mixed sauce evenly over the chicken which is piled up on the serving dish. Sprinkle the 'red oil' evenly over the sauce. The 'red oil' is made (if not available from Chinese food-stores) by simmering 1 tbs. of chopped dried red chilli pepper in 2 tbs. of hot vegetable oil for 5 minutes and then straining.

   This is a good dish to serve as a starter (what we Chinese call a 'wine-drinking dish') for diners to eat with their aperitifs. The diners should actually toss and mix the ingredients in the dish at the table themselves.

Steamed Chicken with Spring Onions

(FOR 3-4 PEOPLE)

2½ lb. (1¼ kilo) chicken
5 tbs. oil

for the marinade
3 bunches spring onions
fresh ginger
2 tbs. salt
2 tbs. wine

Preparation
Wash and dry chicken thoroughly.

Marinade
Chop some of the spring onions.
   Chop ginger.
   Marinade spring onions with wine, ginger and salt for 10 minutes. Rub chicken inside and out with marinade and leave for 1 hour.

Cooking
Put chicken into steamer and steam for about 50 minutes.
   Turn off heat, but leave chicken in steamer for a further 10 minutes.
   Remove chicken from steamer.
   Cut into strips and arrange on a plate like a whole chicken.
   Chop the rest of the spring onions.
   Chop ½ cup of ginger.
   Mix spring onions and ginger and sprinkle over chicken.
   Boil in a pan 5 tbs. oil.
   Pour it over the ginger and onion on the chicken.
   Strain oil from chicken and put it back in pan.
   Heat again and when hot pour over chicken again.
   Repeat this twice more and then throw away oil.

Serving
Serve chicken hot.

The Shangtung Fried and Steamed Hand-Shredded Chicken

(FOR 5-6 PEOPLE)

1 3½ lb. (approx. 1¾ kilo) chicken
4-5 slices root ginger (shredded)
4-5 spring onions (sectioned, chopped)

3 tbs. *coriander leaves (chopped)*
5-6 *pieces anise*
3 tsp. *pepper corns (pounded)*
1½ tsp. *salt*
1½ tbs. *soya sauce*
1½ tbs. *dry sherry*
oil for deep frying

for sauce
3 *cloves garlic*
3 *green chillis*
2 *stalks spring onions*
1 tsp. *sugar*
1 tbs. *sesame oil*
2½ lbs. *chicken stock*
3 tsp. *vinegar*
½ tbs. *'red-oil' (cf. p.00) or chilli sauce*

Preparation
Rub the chicken with all the other ingredients except oil and leave to season for 2½-3 hours.

Cooking
After seasoning, deep fry chicken for 5-6 minutes until somewhat brown. Remove and place in a steamer to steam vigorously for 35-40 minutes. Allow to cool for a few minutes.

Serving
When the chicken is cool enough, hand-tear it with the aid of a knife into large strips or shreds. Reassemble the strips or chicken shreds on a serving dish.

Prepare the following sauce
Finely slice or chop garlic, green chillis and spring onions; stir fry them with sugar, sesame oil, chicken stock and vinegar. Stir quickly over medium heat for 20 seconds and pour the contents over the chicken with ½ tbs. 'red-oil' (red-chilli oil, see p. 53) and serve.

Quick-Fried Diced Chicken Cubes with Cucumber (in garlic sauce)

(FOR 4-5 PEOPLE)

½ lb. (225g.) breast of chicken
3 tbs. cornflour
1 tsp. salt
1 egg white
½ medium cucumber
2-3 cloves garlic
4 tbs. vegetable oil
1½ tbs. lard (or oil)

for sauce
2 slices root ginger
4 tbs. chicken stock
2 tbs. water (blended with 3 tsp. cornflour)
½ tsp. taste powder (optional) or ½ chicken stock cube

Preparation
Cut chicken into sugar-lump-sized cubes. Dust and rub with salt and cornflour, and wet with egg white. Cut cucumber (including skin) into similar-sized cubes. Crush garlic and shred ginger.

Cooking
Heat oil in frying pan or wok. When hot add the chicken. Break it up into individual pieces, turn and stir them in the pan over high heat for 1½ minutes, then remove and put aside.

Add lard or oil to the pan together with garlic and ginger. Stir them around together for 15 seconds and pour in the chicken stock. Continue to stir for 10 seconds. Remove the ginger and garlic with perforated spoon. Add the cucumber and return the chicken to the pan. Stir and turn until the contents are well heated through. Add water blended with cornflour, taste powder or crumbled stock cube. Stir and turn them all together for a further 15 seconds.

Serving
Serve on a well-heated serving dish; eat hot.

Onion 'Blasted' Boiled Chicken

(FOR 8 PEOPLE)

1 medium 3½ lb. (approx. 1¾ kilo) young chicken

for boiling
1 tbs. salt
4-5 slices root ginger
1-2 large onions

for garnish and sauce
3 spring onions
3 slices root ginger
2 cloves garlic
2 tbs. soya sauce
2 tbs. dry sherry
5 tbs. vegetable oil

Preparation
Bring saucepanful of water to boil. Add sliced onions, ginger and salt.
Cut spring onions and ginger into fine shreds, and chop garlic finely. Clean chicken thoroughly.

Cooking and serving
Add chicken to the pan of water in which onion and ginger are boiling. Bring contents to quick boil, and simmer for 25 minutes. Turn heat off and, when slightly cool, lift out the chicken and chop it on a chopping board through bone into 20 bite-sized pieces. Reassemble and lay the chicken pieces out evenly on a heatproof serving dish. Pour soya sauce and sherry evenly over the chicken. Spread the minced garlic and shredded ginger and spring onion evenly over the top of the chicken.
Heat oil in a small pan or metal ladle until it smokes and is very hot. Pour the oil evenly over chicken pieces covered with shredded spring onions and ginger (the action is almost like a explosion on impact). Pour the liquid which has accumulated at the bottom of the dish into a pan to re-heat until it is very hot. Pour this liquid once more over the layer of shredded spring onions and ginger onto the chicken. Serve hot.

Deep-Fried Boneless Duck

(FOR 6-8 PEOPLE)

1 pint 'master sauce' (25% soya sauce, 75% good stock, 4 cloves
garlic, 2½ tsp. five-spice powder)
1 duck (about 3½ lb./approx. 1¾ kilos)
3-4 pieces anise
1 egg
3-4 tbs. cornflour with 2½ tbs. self-raising flour
oil for deep frying

Preparation
Parboil duck in a large pan of boiling water for 4-5 minutes and
drain. Mix egg, cornflour and self-raising flour into a consistent
batter.

Cooking and serving
Mix ingredients of 'master sauce' and heat with anise in a
saucepan or casserole. Add duck. Turn it over in the sauce a few
times, and leave to simmer for 40 minutes, turning the bird over
every 10 minutes.
   Remove the duck and drain thoroughly. Remove the bones of the
duck, which can be done quite easily now it is cooked. Turn the
pieces of duck in the batter until they are evenly coated.
   Immerse the battered duck in boiling oil for 7-8 minutes. Drain
and cut duck into large bite-sized pieces. Arrange on a serving dish
and serve. (In China the meat is sometimes reassambled into shape
of a duck before serving.) In our restaurant it is eaten wrapped in
lettuce leaves brushed with Peking Duck sauce.

Deep-Fried Boneless Chicken

The preceding duck dish can be made with chicken, by simply
substituting chicken for duck. Indeed chicken often provides more
meat; its lack of flavour these days is made good by the long
braising in 'master sauce'. When served the dish should be
accompanied by at least 2-3 dips, including: plum-sauce, Peking
duck sauce (see p. 62) and a blending of soya sauce with chilli-
sauce.

Boneless Duck with Eight Precious Stuffing

(FOR 8-10 PEOPLE)

1 whole duck (4-5 lb./2-2½ kilos)
3 cups glutinous rice (cooked)
4-5 Chinese dried mushrooms
¼ lb. diced ham (cooked or uncooked)
2 tbs. diced bamboo shoots
20 lotus seeds (soaked & cleaned)
1 duck gizzard (boiled)
1 tbs. chopped dried shrimps (soaked)
8 dried chestnuts (soaked)
2 tbs. oil
2 tbs. chopped spring onions
2 tbs. chopped ginger
2 tbs. wine
2 tbs. soya sauce (pale)
½ tsp. salt
pinch black pepper
2 tbs. soya sauce
1 tbs. sugar

Preparation

Clean the duck, using a sharp knife to cut the membranes around the duck's neck downwards between meat and bones; stretch and remove all the bones from the duck and keep it in shape.

Soften the black mushrooms in warm water, and do the same with the dried chestnuts; remove the little green central parts of the lotus seeds, and soak them. Cook the chestnuts and lotus seeds for few minutes until soft.

Heat 2 tbs. of oil, put the chopped spring onions and ginger in first, and follow with diced mushrooms, duck gizzard, lotus seeds, diced ham, shrimps, bamboo shoots and chestnuts; stir in wine, soya sauce, salt and pepper. Stir constantly, turn off the heat, put in the cooked glutinous rice and mix them all well together (this is the stuffing).

Pack the stuffing mixture into the duck cavity and close up the tail opening with a needle and thread, and also repair any torn skin if necessary (the stuffing must not be too full).

Cooking and serving

Pre-heat the oven to gas mark 4 (180°C; 350°F). Rub dry the duck with a towel or tissue paper, brush it with dark soya sauce, place on a wire tray on the top of a baking tin, and put in the oven. Roast for one hour.

Put the cooked duck on a large plate, score the breast with a long central cut, cut both sides into small pieces and sprinkle with chopped spring onions, and serve it hot.

Aromatic and Crispy Duck

(FOR 5-6 PEOPLE)

1 3½ lb. (approx. 1¾ kilos) duckling

cooking sauce
2 pints stock
8 tbs. sugar
4 slices root ginger
oil for deep frying
12 tbs. soya sauce
3 tsp. salt
3 tbs. dry sherry
6 pieces anise
pepper (to taste)

pancakes
6 oz. (170g.) plain flour
spring onions
cucumber

duck sauce
4-5 tbs. sugar
4-5 tbs. yellow bean paste
1 tbs. sesame paste

Preparation and cooking
Heat the ingredients for the cooking sauce together in a large pan. After cleaning the duck, cut in two down from the back. Put them into the sauce to cook, and simmer gently for 3 hours. Lift the duck out of the pan to drain and cool.

When about to serve, deep fry the duck for 10-12 minutes over medium heat until quite crispy, and drain. Serve by scraping the meat from the duck bones, and then wrapping it in pancakes, with shredded spring onions and cucumber.

Pancakes

Add enough hot water slowly into 6 oz. plain flour to blend into a firm dough. Leave the dough for 10 minutes, and form it into a foot long strip. Pinch or break off the strip into 10-12 pieces. Roll the pieces into small balls. Flatten the balls into 6"-7" pancakes.

Place the pancakes one at a time in a dry frying-pan to heat over medium heat until they begin to bubble, and some brown spots appear. Turn over to cook for ¾ minute. Repeat until all the pancakes are cooked.

Serving

Serve by brushing the pancakes with a teaspoon or more of 'duck sauce' and wrapping the duck meat with shredded cucumber and spring onions in the pancake.

The 'duck sauce' is made by simply adding sugar to yellow bean paste and sesame paste, and stirring them together in a small saucepan for 2-3 minutes over low/medium heat.

The Peking Duck

(FOR 6 PEOPLE)

This 'Peking Duck' of Madam Fei's is distinguished by its total simplicity. Madam Fei says 'The simpler the better.'

1 3-4 lb. (1½-2 kilos) duck
½ medium cucumber
½ bundle spring onions
sesame oil

for sauce
small can of yellow bean paste
2-3 tbs. sugar (to taste)
corn oil

for pancakes
1 lb.(450g.) plain flour
1½ tsp. sugar
1 tsp. oil

Preparation

Clean and dry the duck. Hang it up in a breezy spot to dry the skin, for 3 hours or more, or overnight (if in a hurry use a hair-drier on it!).

Clean and cut spring onions into matchstick strips. Cut

cucumber into similar strips.

Cooking
Pre-heat the oven to gas mark 6 (200°C; 400°F). Place the duck on a wire tray set on top of a roasting pan, and put it in the oven. Leave the duck to roast for one hour and 5 minutes (slightly longer — 10 minutes — if the oven proves leaky and less hot than its set temperature). Do not open the oven — the duck requires no basting. After 1 hour 10 minutes the duck should be ready.

Preparing the sauce
Heat 2 tbs. oil in a small saucepan. Add the small can of yellow bean sauce. Stir them together for 2 minutes over low/medium heat. Add the sugar (2-3 tbs. or according to taste). Stir the ingredients together for a further 2-3 minutes over low heat.

Preparing the pancakes
Sift the flour into a mixing bowl. Stir in the sugar, oil and a cup of warm water. Stir and mix with a pair of chopsticks or wooden spoon until well mixed. Knead the mixture into a firm dough and form into 2 large strips. Cut each strip into 10 or 12 pieces and form each piece into a small ball. Flatten each ball with the palm of the hand into a round disc. Brush the top of one of the discs with sesame oil, and place a second disc on top to form a 'sandwich'. Use a small rolling-pin to roll the 'sandwich' into a pancake of about 5"-6" diameter. Repeat until you have used up all the dough-balls and made them into 'sandwich' pancakes.

Cooking the pancakes
Heat a dry frying pan over low/medium heat. When hot place a 'sandwich' pancake on the pan, and shake the latter so that the pancake slides around on the surface of the pan. After $1\frac{1}{2}$ minutes turn the pancake over with a fish-slice and cook the other side in the same manner, until the pancake begins to puff and bubble slightly. The pancake is ready when some brown spots begin to appear on the underside. Now very gently peel the 'sandwich' apart into its two constituent pancakes. Fold each pancake in half, uncooked side inwards, and stack them up. If they are not to be used immediately, cover them with a damp cloth. They can be heated up by placing them in a steamer for a couple of minutes.

Serving and eating
Peking Duck is served, as we all know, by cutting and peeling off the skin of the duck in about $1\frac{1}{2}$" to 2" slices with a sharp knife and serving on a well-heated dish; the meat of the duck is then carved into similar sized pieces, and served on a separate dish.
   The duck skin and meat are eaten by wrapping them in the

pancakes, which are first all brushed with a teaspoon of 'duck sauce' (see p. 62) with a large pinch each of shredded cucumber and spring onions. After wrapping up the duck skin and meat and the vegetables firmly in the pancake, turn up the lower end of the pancake (so that nothing will drop out of it) before eating the stuffed pancake in your fingers.

牛肉

4. Beef

Cantonese Quick-Fried Beef in Oyster Sauce

(FOR 4-5 PEOPLE)

1¼ lb. (565g.) beef steak (topside, rump, sirloin or fillet)
4 tbs. vegetable oil
1 egg
1 tsp. salt
¼ tsp. taste powder (optional)
1½ tbs. cornflour

for sauce
2 spring onions
2 slices root ginger
1 tbs. stock
½ tbs. light soya sauce
1½ tbs. oyster sauce
½ tsp. salt
1 tsp. sugar
1½ tsp. sesame oil
1 tbs. cornflour (blended in 2½ tbs. water)
¼ lb. mange touts (snow peas)

Preparation
Cut beef into 1½" x 1" very thin slices. Sprinkle and rub with salt and taste powder (optional). Mix cornflour with egg and ½ tbs. oil until well blended. Turn the sliced beef in the mixture until evenly coated.

Top and tail the mange touts and clean thoroughly. Cut spring onions into 2" sections and ginger into fine shreds. Mix the other ingredients together into a 'cooking sauce'.

Cooking and serving
Heat frying pan or wok for 10 seconds. Add oil and when hot remove pan from heat and add pieces of beef. Stir them and turn over several times. Replace pan over heat and continue to stir fry

for ½ minute. Remove the beef with perforated spoon and put aside.
    Add spring onions and ginger to the pan. Stir them around a couple of times, over medium heat. Add mange touts and stir fry them all together for ¼ minute. Push them to the sides. Pour the 'cooking sauce' into the middle of the pan and add the beef for ¼ minute. Bring in the mange touts and spring onions. Turn and stir fry all the ingredients together for ½ minute. Serve, and eat hot.

Cantonese Quick-Fried Sliced Beef in Black Bean Sauce

(FOR 5-6 PEOPLE)

1¼ lb. (565g.) beef steak (topside, rump, fillet or sirloin)
1 egg
1 tsp. salt
2 tsp. (finely chopped) root ginger
1½ tbs. cornflour
½ tbs. vegetable oil

for sauce
1½ tbs. salted black beans
1 medium onion
2-3 chilli peppers
1 medium sweet pepper
1 tbs. soya sauce
3 tbs. good stock
1 tbs. cornflour (blended in 2½ tbs. water)
5½ tbs. vegetable oil

Preparation
Cut beef into 2″ x 1″ thin slices. Sprinkle and rub with salt and finely chopped ginger. Mix cornflour with egg and oil until well blended. Add beef to batter and coat evenly.
    Soak black beans in water for 10 minutes. Drain away water. Slice onion thinly. Shred chilli peppers and cut sweet pepper into ¾″ x 1¼″ pieces.

Cooking and serving
Heat 3½ tbs. oil in a frying pan. When hot add the beef and stir fry quickly for 1½ minutes. Remove from pan with perforated spoon and put aside.
    Add rest of oil to the pan, followed by the black beans, sweet

pepper, chilli peppers, stock and soya sauce. Stir them vigorously over high heat for 15 seconds. Add blended cornflour and stir until the sauce is translucent. Return the beef to the pan and turn and stir with the other ingredients for $\frac{1}{2}$ minute. Serve, and eat hot.

Iron-Plate Sizzled Chilli-Beef with Black Bean Sauce

Repeat the previous recipe, except shorten the last phase of the stir frying from $\frac{1}{2}$ minute to $\frac{1}{4}$ minute. Heat the 'iron-plate' just before bringing to the dining table to give a last minute's cooking by pouring the dish into it just before serving.

Quick-Fried Shredded Soya Beef with Shredded Onion

(FOR 4-5 PEOPLE)

1 lb. (450g.) beef steak (topside, rump, sirloin or fillet)
2 medium sized onions
2 slices root ginger
1 tbs. cornflour
$\frac{1}{2}$ egg
2 tsp. vegetable oil
$1\frac{1}{2}$ tbs. soya sauce
$\frac{1}{2}$ tbs. hoisin (also called barbecue) sauce
$\frac{1}{2}$ tbs. yellow bean sauce
$2\frac{1}{2}$ tsp. sugar
5-6 tbs. vegetable oil
1 tbs. dry sherry

Preparation
Slice beef (easier if chilled or frozen first) very thinly. Slice onion and ginger equally thinly. Mix egg with cornflour and oil in a basin, until well blended; add beef to take on an even coating.

Cooking and serving
Heat frying pan or wok for 10 seconds. Add 4-5 tbs. oil and when it is

hot add the onion and ginger. Quick fry them over medium heat for 1½ minutes. Add beef and turn and stir together with the onion and ginger for a further 1½ minutes. Remove with perforated spoon and put aside.

Add remainder of oil to the pan, together with soya sauce, hoisin sauce, sugar, yellow bean sauce and sherry. Stir and mix them into a consistent sauce. Return the beef and onion and ginger to the pan; mix and stir fry with the sauce over high heat for one minute. Serve hot (excellent consumed with rice).

Quick-Fried Sliced Beef with Young Leeks (or spring onions) and Garlic

(FOR 4-5 PEOPLE)

½ lb. (225g.) lean beef
2-3 young leeks (or 4 spring onions)
3 cloves garlic
4 tbs. vegetable oil
1 tsp. sesame oil

for marinading the beef
¾ tsp. salt
½ tbs. dry sherry
1 tbs. vegetable oil
1 tbs. water
1 tbs. cornflour
¼ tsp. pepper

Preparation
Cut beef with sharp knife into 2″ long oblong shaped thin slices. Mix the marinade ingredients and add the beef slices. Leave to season for 10-15 minutes. Cut garlic into thin slices and leeks or spring onion into ¼″ sections.

Cooking
Heat the wok or frying pan until quite hot, and then add the oil. After ¼ minute add the garlic, stir around once or twice, and follow with the beef. Stir fry quickly over high heat until the meat changes colour (about 1½ minutes). Remove and put aside, leaving some oil and sauce still in the pan.

Add the sliced leeks (or spring onions) to the pan. Stir quickly for a matter of 10-15 seconds. Return the meat to the pan and stir and turn together with the vegetables still over high heat. Sprinkle the contents with sesame oil.

Serving
Transfer the contents to a well heated serving dish and consume immediately.

Szechuan Hot-Fried Crispy Shredded Beef

(FOR 4-5 PEOPLE)

¾ lb. (340g.) beef (topside)
4 eggs
¼ lb. (115g.) cornflour
½ tsp. salt
oil for deep frying

for sauce
3 medium carrots
2 spring onions
3 cloves of garlic
2-3 chilli peppers
6 tsp. sugar
3-4 tbs. vinegar
3 tsp. soya sauce

Preparation
Cut beef first into thin slices and then into matchstick strips. Beat the eggs together with salt and cornflour. Add shredded beef and coat with batter.

Clean and cut carrots into similar matchsticks. Cut spring onions into 1½″ sections (divide thicker stalks first lengthwise into halves or quarters).

Shred chillis and chop garlic coarsely.

Cooking and serving
Deep fry beef over a moderate heat for 5 minutes (or until crispy) and drain. Deep fry carrots for 1½ minutes. Pour away the oil from the pan, leaving about 1½ tbs. in the bottom. Add the spring onions, chillis and chopped garlic. Stir fry them together for 1½ minutes

over a medium heat. Add the sugar, soya sauce and vinegar and finally beef.

Turn all ingredients around quickly in the sauce over a high heat for about 15 seconds, and serve.

Cantonese 'Willow-Cut' Beef Steak with Onion

(FOR 4-6 PEOPLE)

1 lb. (450g.) fillet of beef
1 medium onion
1-2 slices root ginger
1½ tsp. salt
1 egg
2 tbs. cornflour
1 tbs. soya sauce
pepper (to taste)
4 tbs. vegetable oil
1 tbs. cornflour (blended in 2½ tbs. water)

for sauce
6 tbs. good stock
1½ tbs. oyster sauce
2-3 tbs. tomato purée
1½ tbs. Worcester sauce (Lea & Perrins sauce)
1 tbs. hoisin sauce

Preparation
Cut beef into ⅔″ x 2½″ 'willow' (long and thin) strips. Sprinkle and rub with salt, soya sauce and pepper (to taste). Mix egg with cornflour. Put beef in batter and turn the mixture to take on a coating of batter. Leave to season for ½ hour. Cut onion into thin slices, and chop ginger finely.

Cooking
Heat frying pan or wok for 10 seconds. Add oil. When hot add the onion and ginger and stir together for 1½ minutes over medium heat. Add stock, tomato purée, oyster sauce, hoisin sauce and Worcester sauce. Stir them together and mix well over high heat. When the liquid has been reduced by ⅓ add the beef and turn it in the sauce for 1½ minutes. Add the blended cornflour and stir with the beef for ¼ minute. Serve, and eat hot.

Soya-Braised Beef with Carrots

(FOR 4-6 PEOPLE)

2 lb. (1 kilo) stewing beef
1 lb. (450g.) carrots
3 tbs. vegetable oil
4 lb. soya sauce
2 tbs. hoisin sauce
1 tbs. sugar
½ pint (290ml.) stock
3 tbs. dry sherry
½ tbs.yellow bean sauce

Preparation
Cut beef into thin 2″ x 1″ oblong pieces. Cut carrots into slightly smaller, similarly shaped pieces.

Cooking and serving
Heat oil in a large casserole. When hot add beef and carrots. Stir them over high heat for a couple of minutes. Add soya sauce, hoisin sauce and yellow bean sauce. Mix with the beef and carrots. When the contents boil, add sugar, sherry and stock. When they re-boil remove the casserole from the top of the cooker and put into a pre-heated oven at gas mark 6 (200°C; 400°F). Thirty minutes later reduce heat to gas mark 1-2 (150°-160°C; 300°-325°F) and leave to cook, covered, for 1½ hours, turning the contents over 2-3 times in the course of the cooking.

When serving, the meat and gravy should be spooned out into the diners' rice-bowls to be consumed with rice.

羊肉

5. Lamb

Mongolian 'Barbecue' of Lamb in Lettuce Puffs

(FOR 10-12 PEOPLE)

1 leg of lamb (about 3½ lb./1¾ kilos meat after boning)
1 tbs. salt
3 tsp. pepper corns
4-5 slices root ginger
4-5 spring onions
2 tbs. soya sauce
1½ tbs. hoisin sauce
oil for deep frying
12 or more lettuce leaves
½ medium size cucumber

sauce
same as Peking duck sauce (cf. p. 62)

Preparation and cooking
Crush the pepper corns and finely slice the ginger and spring onions. After boning the lamb, cut it into half a dozen strips. Sprinkle evenly with salt, soya sauce, hoisin sauce, pepper corns, ginger and spring onions. Leave to season for 1 hour (or longer if time permits). Wrap the seasoned lamb in tinfoil and put it into a steamer on a heatproof dish or pan to steam for 2 hours. Leave to cool until required.

When required deep fry the strips of lamb for 4 minutes. Remove and cut across grain into large bite-sized pieces. -

Serving
Serve the lamb with a dozen or more large pieces of ice-berg lettuce.Use the lettuce leaves to wrap the lamb in the same way as pancakes are used to wrap Peking duck; apply a generous amount of sauce to the meat, add a large pinch of both shredded cucumber and spring onion and roll them all together into a firm roll. Eat it by treating it as if it is a pancake roll.

Sauté of Lamb-Steak with Onion and Ginger

(FOR 4-6 PEOPLE)

1½ lb. (675g.) leg of lamb
1 large onion
4 slices root ginger
salt and pepper (to taste)
½ tbs. yellow bean sauce
1 tbs. soya sauce
1 tbs. hoisin sauce
1½ tbs. dry sherry
4 tbs. vegetable oil
2 spring onions

Preparation
Cut lamb into 2" x 1" and ⅕" thick pieces. Sprinkle and rub with about 1-1½ tsp. salt and pepper (to taste). Mix yellow bean sauce, soya sauce, hoisin sauce, ½ tbs. oil and sherry into a marinade. Apply the marinade to the lamb, and leave to season for an hour. Cut onion into thin pieces, slice ginger thinly and cut spring onions into 2" sections.

Cooking and serving
Heat frying pan or wok and add oil. When hot add the onion and ginger and stir fry over high heat for 1 minute. Reduce heat to medium and stir fry for another minute, then push them to the sides of the pan. Put the lamb pieces into the centre of the pan (spread out in a single layer) and sauté for 1½ minutes on each side. Add the spring onions. Scramble and turn; stir fry all the contents together for 1 minute over high heat and serve.

Mongolian Sliced Lamb Hot-Pot

(FOR 6-8 PEOPLE)

The dish is cooked on the table. It can only be properly cooked and served in a conventional Chinese charcoal hot-pot or in an electric wok.

4 lb. (2 kilo) leg of lamb
4 pints (2½ litres) good stock

1 medium Chinese cabbage (or 1 lb./450g. spinach)
1 lb. (450g.) noodles (poached)
3 spring onions
2 slices root ginger
6 eggs

for dips
4 tbs. dark soya sauce
1 tbs. chilli sauce
3-4 tbs. hoisin sauce
2 tbs. English mustard
3 tbs. light soya sauce
3 tbs. vinegar mixed with 2 tsp. chopped garlic
(two dishfuls of each type in separate dishes)

Preparation
Freeze the lamb and cut with sharp knife into paper-thin 2½" x 1" slices. Cut Chinese white cabbage or young spinach into 2" slices, and spring onions into 1½" sections. Parboil the noodles for a couple of minutes, drain and place in two bowls. Arrange the spinach or cabbage in 2-3 large bowls. Spread the lamb in a single layer over 7-8 medium sized dishes. Arrange over the table-top to the convenience of the diners. Each diner should be provided with a bowl, a small side-plate to rest his spoon in and a long pair of wooden or bamboo chopsticks.

Cooking and eating
With this dish the cooking is done by the diners. Boil the stock in the hot-pot, add the ginger, a handful of spring onions and a bunch of cabbage or spinach. As contents re-boil, add one plateful of sliced lamb. Meanwhile each diner makes up his own 'personal sauce' with the different dips on the table. A minute after the contents have re-boiled he 'fishes' out a piece or two of the lamb together with whatever vegetable is handy, dips them quickly in the sauce and eats them.

Repeat the process but add into hot-pot only a smaller amount of meat at a time than initially; from now on each diner basically looks after his own cooking (since part of the fun is in the cooking). Not infrequently he might break an egg into his own bowl, and dip his freshly cooked lamb into it before applying any sauce.

During cooking and eating the stock in the pot is steadily replenished, and becomes very tasty and savoury (owing to the large amount of meat being cooked in it, each time very quickly and freshly). This is the time for the diners to add the noodles and the remainder of the vegetable into the hot-pot. These will now be allowed to simmer together for 4-5 minutes when they will be ladled out into each diner's bowl to be consumed or gulped down as the necessary bulk food which we Chinese require for our total satisfaction.

Quick-Fried Lamb with Leeks or Spring Onions in Garlic Sauce

(FOR 4-5 PEOPLE)

¾ lb. (340g.) lean lamb (sliced)
½ lb. (225g.) young leeks
2 tbs. oil (to marinate lamb)
1 tbs. soy sauce
½ tsp. salt
1 tbs. wine or sherry
¼ tsp. freshly ground pepper
½ tsp. cornflour
3 tbs. chopped garlic
1 tbs. vinegar
1 tbs. good stock
1 tbs. sesame oil
6 tbs. cooking oil

Preparation
Choose lean and tender lamb and slice it very thin; it will be easier to slice when half frozen. Place the sliced meat in a bowl and marinate it with 2 tbs. oil for at least 30 minutes.

Cut leeks first lengthwise into halves, and then diagonally into 2″ sections. Mix together soy sauce, salt, vinegar, wine, pepper, cornflour and sesame oil in a small bowl for later use.

Cooking
Heat frying pan or wok over high heat for 20 seconds, then add 6 tbs. of cooking oil and wait until it starts to smoke. Add chopped garlic first, then lamb. Stir fry meat very quickly over high heat for 15 seconds; pour away excess oil. Add leeks and seasoning sauce and continue to stir fry quickly for 25 seconds. Serve immediately.

Note
The secret of the success of this dish is to use high heat and to cook with speed.

猪肉

6. Pork

Lotus-Leaf-Wrapped Aromatic Steamed Pork

(FOR 6-8 PEOPLE)

2-2½ lb. (1-1¼ kilos) belly of pork
½ lb. (225g.) rice
2½ tbs. dark soya sauce
1½ tbs. hoisin sauce
½ tbs. sugar
2 tbs. dry sherry
2 slices root ginger
1 clove garlic
1-2 sheets of lotus leaves (dried)
2 feet tinfoil

Preparation
Cut pork through skin into approximately 2½″ x 1½″ lean and fat pieces. Chop ginger and garlic finely. Mix them with soya sauce, hoisin sauce, sherry and sugar. Add the mixture to the pork in a basin and stir them together thoroughly. Leave them in the basin to season for one hour or more.

Meanwhile place the rice in a dry small frying pan. Stir fry it over low heat for 2-3 minutes or until aromatic and brown. Turn heat off and leave rice to dry further in the pan. Place the rice in a mortar and grind coarsely. Add this aromatic rice to the pork and mix so that each piece of meat is evenly covered.

Soak the lotus leaves in water for 3 minutes to soften. Wipe to dry and tip the pork into the middle of a lotus leaf and wrap it up carefully (if necessary use a second leaf to complete the wrapping). To hold the leaf-wrapped parcel firmly together use a large sheet of tinfoil as the outer wrapping, so that the parcel will not loosen and open during the process of cooking.

Cooking and serving
Place the well wrapped 'parcel' of pork in a steamer and steam steadily for 3-3½ hours.

Place the 'parcel' in a large serving dish and bring it to the dining table. Unwrap the 'parcel' in view of the diners, who should ladle large spoonfuls of the pork directly onto the rice in their rice bowls. This is a favourite Chinese 'family-cooked' food and should be eaten unceremoniously.

Double-Cooked Pork

(FOR 4-5 PEOPLE)

1 lb. (450g.) neck of pork (or lean belly of pork)
1 green pepper
2-3 leaves Chinese cabbage
1 tbs. yellow bean paste
4 tbs. vegetable oil
2 spring onions
2 cloves garlic
½ tsp. dark soya sauce
1½ tbs. sugar

Preparation
Boil pork for ½ hour. Cut pork into 1½" x 1½" thin slices. Cut cabbage into similar sized pieces, pepper into pieces half the size and spring onions into ½" long sections. Crush garlic.

Cooking and serving
Heat oil in a frying pan. When hot add the pork pieces; stir fry them over high heat for 3 minutes and remove with perforated spoon. Reduce heat to low and add garlic, yellow bean paste, soya sauce and sugar. Stir and mix them in the remaining oil for ½ minute. Return the pork to the pan, together with the cabbage, spring onions and pepper. Raise the heat to high, stir and turn all the ingredients together at a brisk pace for 2 minutes. Serve on a well heated serving dish.

Mu Shu Rou

(FOR 5-6 PEOPLE)

½ lb. (225g.) minced pork
3 eggs
2 spring onions
1-1½ oz. (25-40g.) wood ears
5 tbs. vegetable oil
2 slices root ginger
salt (to taste)
pepper (to taste)
1 tbs. soya sauce
¼ tsp. taste powder

Preparation

Add soya sauce, ¼ tsp. salt and pepper (to taste), taste powder and 2
tsp. water to minced pork in a mixing bowl. Mix and blend them
well together. Leave to season for 10-15 minutes.

Wash and soak the wood ears in a bowl of water for 15 minutes
and drain. Beat eggs lightly in a bowl or cup with ¼ tsp. of salt.
Wash and cut spring onions into 1½" sections.

Cooking

Heat 3 tbs. oil in a frying pan. When hot add the ginger, stir fry for a
minute and remove. Add the seasoned pork and stir fry for 3
minutes. Add the wood ears and spring onions and continue to stir
fry for 2 minutes and remove from heat.

Heat the remaining oil in a smaller frying pan. When hot pour in
the beaten eggs. When set, add the egg to the pork in the larger pan.
Fluff and stir fry them together for 1½ minutes and serve.

Serving

The Mu Shu Rou can be eaten by wrapping it in pancakes in the
same way as Peking duck (add duck sauce, p. 62, if you want to). Or
it can be eaten with rice and served together with other savoury
dishes on the table.

Long-Cooked Soya-Braised Knuckle of Pork

(FOR 5-6 PEOPLE)

This is to be eaten with plain boiled rice and one vegetable dish.

1 knuckle pork (about 3-4 lb./1½-2 kilos)
5½ tbs. soya sauce (dark)
3-4 heads star anise
2-3 slices root ginger
1 large onion
1 tbs. sugar
1½ tsp. salt
1½ pints (1 litre) chicken stock

for sauce
4-5 Chinese dried mushrooms
2-3 oz. (55-85g.) bamboo shoots
½ chicken stock cube
2-3 tbs. dry sherry
1½ heaped tbs. cornflour

Preparation
Clean knuckle of pork and put in a pan of boiling water to simmer for 20 minutes. Drain and rub the knuckle with 2 tbs. of soya sauce. Leave to season for ½ hour.

Deep fry the knuckle (or shallow fry by turning it in a smaller amount of oil) for 8-10 minutes until it is quite brown.

Soak mushrooms in warm water for 20 minutes, then remove stems. Cut bamboo shoots into 2″ x 1″ slices.

Cooking and serving
Heat chicken stock in a deep frying pan or casserole. When hot add the knuckle, together with the ginger, sliced onion, anise, sugar, soya sauce and salt. Cover the casserole and leave to cook gently at gas mark 3 (160°C; 325°F) for the next two hours in a pre-heated oven. Turn the knuckle once every ½-¾ hour.

Remove the knuckle and place it in a deep-sided dish. Place the casserole on top of a cooker. Add dried mushrooms, bamboo shoots and crushed chicken stock cube. Reduce the sauce over high heat to about half. Add sherry and cornflour which have been blended in 3-4 tbs. water, and stir for about 2-3 minutes, for the gravy to thicken. Pour the sauce over the knuckle and serve.

The knuckle is frequently served by surrounding it with a quantity of quick-fried green vegetables, such as mange touts, French beans or spinach.

Cha Siu Roast Pork (flavoured with red bean curd cheese)

(FOR 4-6 PEOPLE)

1½ lb. (675g.) fillet of pork
1½ tbs. red 'bean curd cheese'
1½ tbs. soya sauce
3 tsp. vegetable oil
2 tsp. sugar
3 tsp. yellow wine (Chinese rice wine or dry sherry)

Preparation
Mix all ingredients except pork into a marinade. Rub the marinade on the pork and allow the latter to season in the marinade for an hour.

Cooking
Place the marinated pork on a wire rack over a roasting pan and put it into a pre-heated oven (gas mark 6: 200°C; 400°F) to bake at this high heat for 13-15 minutes.

Serving
Remove from oven. Cut pork across grain into ⅕" thick slices. Serve immediately, using the drippings in the pan under the wire rack as gravy or sauce.

'Pearl' Studded Meat-Balls

(FOR 5-6 PEOPLE)

1 lb. (450g.) minced pork
1 egg
2 tbs. ground dried shrimps
1 tbs. finely chopped onion
1½ tsp. finely chopped root ginger
½ tbs. salt
1 tbs. soya sauce (light colour)
2 tbs. cornflour
½ lb. (225g.) glutinous rice

Preparation
Soak rice for ½ hour and drain thoroughly. Place pork in a large mixing bowl. Add 2 tbs. water. Add all the other ingredients except rice and cornflour. Beat and mix well until the mixture is consistent.

Sprinkle a large flat plate or tray with a thin layer of cornflour (about 1½ tbs.) and spread the glutinous rice evenly on top. Turn and mix the rice with the cornflour.

Form the meat mixture into 20 meat-balls. Wet them lightly with warm water. Place these meat-balls on top of the glutinous rice. Tilt the tray or plate back and forth so that the balls will take on a covering of rice; pick the meat-balls up individually and roll them into rounder balls, pressing additional rice onto patches of the meat-balls which are not completely covered by rice.

Cooking and serving
Place the completely covered meat-balls one by one spaced out in a steam-basket, the bottom of which is covered with muslin (or cloth). Bring water to a high boil and steam vigorously for 25 minutes.

Serve on a well heated serving dish, using good quality soya sauce, ketchup, and other mixed sauces as dips.

Quick-Fried 'Kidney Flower' with Cauliflower

(FOR 4 PEOPLE)

3-4 pork or lamb's kidneys'
1 medium cauliflower
¾ tbs. cornflour (blended in 2½ tbs. water)
oil for deep frying or semi deep frying

for marinade
1 tsp. sugar
2 tbs. dry sherry
½ tbs. vegetable oil
1 tsp. salt
½ tbs. hoisin sauce
2 tbs. soya sauce

Preparation
Remove the membrane and the gristle from the kidneys. Cut each kidney into 4 strips and slash each strip halfway through in a criss-

cross fashion half a dozen times. Add the marinade ingredients to the kidneys and leave to season for 20 minutes. Break the cauliflower into individual flowerets.

Cooking
Heat ½ pint oil in a frying pan. When hot (test with crumb) add the cauliflower flowerets. Stir them in the hot oil for 1½ minutes. Remove and drain. Add the kidney pieces and turn and stir fry in the oil for ½ minute (reserving the remainder of the marinade). Remove and drain. Pour away the oil and add the balance of marinade to the pan. Return both the kidney and cauliflower to the pan.
Stir them around quickly. After half a minute, add the blended cornflour to mix with other materials in the pan. Turn and mix for ½ minute.

Serving
Serve in a well-heated dish and eat hot.

Sweet and Sour Pork

(FOR 4-5 PEOPLE)

2 lb. (1 kilo) lean and fat pork (rib, fillet of pork, or leaner part of belly)
1 egg
1 tsp. salt
3 tbs. cornflour
3 tbs. self-raising flour
oil for deep frying or semi deep frying
2 slices of pineapple

for sauce (to be blended together)
2 tbs. sugar
3 tbs. vinegar
3 tbs. tomato purée
3 tbs. orange juice
1½ tbs. soya sauce
1½ tbs. cornflour (blended in 4 tbs. water)

Preparation
Mix cornflour, self-raising flour, salt and egg into a consistent batter. Cut pork into 2½″ x 1½″ oblong pieces, 1″ thick. Add them to

the batter in a basin to take on an even coating. Mix the sauce ingredients in a basin into a smooth sauce. Cut pineapple into sugar-lump-sized pieces.

Cooking
Heat oil in a pan or deep-fryer until a crumb will sizzle when dropped into it; add the pieces of battered pork to deep fry in it for 3-$3\frac{1}{2}$ minutes. Remove and drain (put aside just for 2-3 minutes).

Prepare the sauce by heating 2 tbs. of oil in a frying pan. Add the pineapple pieces and the mixed sauce. Stir over medium heat until the sauce thickens and becomes translucent. Lower the pork pieces once more into the hot oil for another 1-$1\frac{1}{2}$ minutes' deep frying. Remove and drain and transfer them into the pan containing the sweet and sour sauce. Stir and turn the pork pieces in the sauce over medium heat, until every piece is well covered.

Serving
Serve hot on a well heated dish (either for wine-drinking or to accompany rice).

Quick-Fry of 'Three Types of Cubed Meats'

(FOR 4-5 PEOPLE)

$\frac{1}{2}$ lb. (225g.) fillet of pork
$\frac{1}{3}$ lb. (150g.) pork liver
$\frac{1}{3}$ lb. (150g.) pork kidneys (or 3 lamb's kidneys)
2 cloves garlic
1 tbs. cornflour
2 slices ginger
oil for deep frying (or 9-10 tbs. for semi deep frying)

for sauce
$1\frac{1}{2}$ tbs. soya sauce
$\frac{1}{2}$ tbs. yellow bean paste
1 tbs. hoisin sauce
$\frac{1}{2}$ tbs. sugar
2 tbs. dry sherry
$\frac{1}{2}$ tbs. tomato purée
$\frac{1}{2}$ tbs. cornflour (blended in 2 tbs. water)

Preparation
Cut pork and liver into small sugar-lump-sized pieces. Remove the membrane and gristle from the kidneys and cut into similar sized pieces. Dust evenly with cornflour and wet and rub with 1 tbs. oil. Mix the sauce ingredients together until well blended. Crush the garlic slightly.

Cooking
If a frying pan is used, heat oil in it until a crumb will sizzle when dropped into it. Add the garlic and ginger and fry in it to flavour the oil for ½ minute; remove with perforated spoon and discard. Add the pork cubes first and stir around ¼ minute, then add liver, followed by the kidneys. Turn and stir them in the hot oil over high heat for 1½ minutes. Remove and drain.

Pour away all the oil except for 1½-2 tbs. Add the sauce ingredients to the pan. Stir and blend them together at the bottom of the pan to form a thick creamy sauce. Return the pork cubes, liver and kidney to the pan and turn, stir and mix with the sauce for ½ minute over high heat.

Serving
Serve hot on a well heated dish (either for wine-drinking or to accompany rice).

Fukien Onion-Smothered Pork Chops

(FOR 4-5 PEOPLE)

2½ lb. (1-1¼ kilos)
1 tsp. salt
pepper to taste
1 tbs. soya sauce
1½ tbs. hoisin sauce
2 tsp. sugar
3 medium onions
4 tbs. vegetable oil
3 slices root ginger
3-4 spring onions
½ pint (290 ml.) stock or water
3 tbs. dry sherry

Preparation
Chop each pork chop into 3 pieces (each with bone attached).

Sprinkle with salt and pepper, and rub with 1 tbs. oil. Cut onion into thin slices. Chop ginger finely and cut spring onions into 2-3" sections.

Cooking
Heat wok or large saucepan and add remainder of oil. When hot add the ginger and onion, and stir fry over medium heat for 2-3 minutes. Add all the pieces of pork chops. Stir and turn with the onions. Add the soya sauce, hoisin sauce and sugar. Continue to stir and turn until well mixed with all the other ingredients. Leave to simmer for 3-4 minutes. Turn and stir once more, and add the stock (or water). When the contents re-boil, transfer them into a medium sized casserole. Put the casserole into a pre-heated oven at 200°C (gas mark 6; 400°F).

After 30 minutes turn the contents over and reduce heat to 150°-160°C (gas mark 1-2; 300°-325°F). Leave the casserole in the oven at this temperature for 1½ hours.

Open the casserole. Add the spring onions and sherry. Place the casserole on top of the cooker on medium heat. Turn the contents in the casserole over several times.

Serving
Bring the casserole to the dining table. An excellent dish to consume with rice.

Fukien Anchovy Pork

(FOR 4-5 PEOPLE)

Repeat the previous recipe, using 2½ lb. (1-1¼ kilos) belly of pork (cut to approximately 2½" x 1½" x 1" pieces, each with skin attached). After the pork has been in the oven for 30 minutes at 200°C (gas mark 6; 400°F), add 1 small can of anchovy fillets and distribute the contents evenly over the pork; continue to cook as in previous recipe for 1¼ hours. Serve in the same manner to consume with plain boiled rice.

Szechuan 'Yu Hsiang' Pork Ribbons Quick-Fried with Shredded Vegetables

(FOR 4-5 PEOPLE)

¾ lb. (340g.) lean pork
3 slices root ginger
2-3 cloves garlic
2-3 oz. (55-85g.) Szechuan Hot Ja Chai pickle
⅓ lb. (150g.) snow peas (or mange touts)
⅓ lb. (150g.) white cabbage
1 red pepper
2 medium young carrots
2 dried chilli peppers
3-4 oz. (85-115g.) bean sprouts
4 tbs. vegetable oil
1 tsp. salt
2-3 tsp. sesame oil
4 tbs. stock

for sauce
2½ tbs. soya sauce
1½ tbs. hoisin sauce
1 tbs. 'red oil' (or chilli sauce)
1½ tbs. vinegar

Preparation
Cut pork first of all into very thin slices, and then into 1″-1½″ long pieces. Cut ginger, snow peas, cabbage, peppers and carrots into similar slices. Mix the sauce ingredients. Crush garlic.

Cooking
Heat oil in frying pan or wok. When hot, add dried pepper, Ja Chai pickle, pork and ginger. Stir them around for 1½ minutes over high heat and add all the other shredded vegetables and garlic. Sprinkle contents with salt and continue to stir and turn them around for 2 minutes. Add stock and continue with the turning and stirring for a further 2 minutes. Add the sauce mixture and sesame oil for a final 2 more minutes of stir frying together and serve.

Serving
Serve on a well heated dish for consumption with rice. This is a pronouncedly spicy dish which is characteristic of the food and cooking of Szechuan.

Quick-Fried Sliced Pork Liver with Onion Sautéed in Sweet and Sour Sauce

(FOR 4-5 PEOPLE)

1 lb. (450g.) pork liver
2 medium onions
1½ tbs. soya sauce
½ tbs. yellow bean sauce
½ tbs. hoisin sauce
½ tbs. oyster sauce
4 tbs. vegetable oil

for sweet and sour sauce
1 tbs. sugar
2 tbs. wine vinegar
1 tsp. tomato purée
2 tbs. orange juice
½ tbs. soya sauce
1 tbs. cornflour (blended in 3 tbs. water)

Preparation
Cut liver into 2½" x 1½" thin slices. Add soya sauce, yellow bean sauce, hoisin sauce, ½ tbs. oil and oyster sauce; rub and marinate together. Leave to season for 1 hour. Cut onion into thin slices. Mix sweet and sour ingredients into a well blended sauce.

Cooking and serving
Heat wok or frying pan and add oil. When hot, add the sliced liver piece by piece well spread out on the bottom of the pan to sauté for 1½ minutes on the one side and for 1 minute on the other over medium heat. Remove with fish slice and put aside.

Add onion and stir fry in the remainder of oil for 3 minutes. Push them aside and return the liver to the pan. Stir and turn the liver together with the onions for ½ minutes. Pour the sweet and sour mixture over them to mix with the liver and onion for 1 minute. Serve hot.

Peking Deep Fried and Stir Fried Shredded Pork

(FOR 4-5 PEOPLE)

1 lb. (450g.) lean pork
1 egg
2 tbs. cornflour (blended with 2 tbs. water)
1 tbs. self-raising flour
oil for deep frying (or semi deep frying)

for stir frying and seasoning
3 spring onions
2 cloves garlic
3 slices root ginger
1-2 chilli peppers
2 tsp. sesame oil
1½ tsp. salt and pepper to taste
1 tbs. dry sherry
2 tbs. stock
¼ tbs. vinegar
½ tsp. taste powder (optional)

Preparation
Cut pork into 2″ long double matchstick thick shreds. Beat egg and mix with blended cornflour and self-raising flour into a batter. Add and mix with the pork.

Cut spring onions into 1½″ long slices, and ginger and chilli pepper into fine slices. Crush garlic.

Cooking
Heat oil until a crumb will sizzle when dropped into it. Add the battered shredded pork to fry in it until crispy (about 3½ minutes). Remove and drain.

Heat 3 tbs. oil in a frying pan or wok. Add garlic, ginger, spring onions, chilli pepper and stir fry in it over high heat for ½ minute. Add sherry, vinegar, stock, taste powder, salt and freshly ground pepper. Stir them together a few times.

Add the battered shredded pork and turn and stir quickly with other ingredients over high heat for ½ minute.

Serving
Serve on a well heated dish (excellent for consuming with wine).

Cantonese Steamed Pork Spare Ribs in Black Bean Sauce

(FOR 4-5 PEOPLE)

2 lb. (1 kilo) spare ribs
3 cloves garlic
2 spring onions
2 dried chilli peppers
3 tsp. sugar
1 tsp. salt
3 tsp. sesame oil
2 tbs. salted black beans
1 tbs. soya sauce
3 tsp. vegetable oil
1 tbs. cornflour (blended in 2½ tbs. water)

Preparation
Chop spare ribs into 1½″ sections, sprinkle with salt. Soak black beans in water for ¼ hour and drain. Chop garlic, spring onions and chilli pepper finely. Add them to the black beans along with soya sauce, sherry, blended cornflour, oil, taste powder (optional), and sesame oil. Mix them together until well blended. Add the mixture to the spare ribs, and thoroughly rub the mixture into the ribs. Leave them to season for ½-1 hour.

Cooking
Place the marinated ribs in a heatproof dish or bowl, and put them into a pre-heated steamer; steam vigorously for 20 minutes.

Serving
Often served as a tea-house snack in China, or to accompany wine. There is a freshness of taste to the seasoned ribs which is appealing.

Steamed 'Pork Pudding'

(FOR 4-5 PEOPLE)

1 lb. (450g.) minced pork
1½ tsp. salt
½ tbs. yellow bean sauce
1½ tbs. soya sauce

pepper to taste
1 medium onion
1-2 cloves garlic
3 water chestnuts
3 tsp. vegetable oil
1 egg
1 small/medium cauliflower

Preparation

Chop garlic finely; chop onion and water chestnuts coarsely. Beat egg lightly. Add all these to the minced pork in a basin. Add salt, yellow bean sauce, soya sauce, pepper and oil. Mix them all together until fairly consistent. Break the cauliflower into individual flowerets.

Cooking

Place the cauliflower at the bottom of a heatproof basin. Pack the seasoned minced pork evenly on top. Insert the basin into a steamer, and steam vigorously for ¾ hour.

Serving

Serve by bringing the heatproof basin to the table. Diners help themselves by spooning minced pork and cauliflower on to the top of their own bowls of rice. A favourite dish of Chinese home-cooking, often served in a large 4-5″ diameter bamboo section, which serves both as a container for steaming as well as a rustic serving bowl.

Quick-Fried Shredded Pork Stir-Fried with Transparent Pea-Starched Noodles and Celery

(FOR 4-6 PEOPLE)

¾ lb. (340g.) lean pork
3-4 oz. (85-115g.) transparent noodles
3 stalks celery
2 spring onions
1½ tsp. salt, and pepper to taste
1 clove garlic
4 tbs. vegetable oil

for sauce
2 tbs. soya sauce
3 tbs. stock
2 tsp. chilli sauce
1½ tbs. vinegar
1½ tbs. dry sherry
2 tsp. sesame oil

Preparation
Cut pork into matchsticks. Sprinkle and rub with salt and pepper. Soak noodles in water for 10 minutes and drain. Cut spring onions in 2″ sections, and celery into similar pieces. Crush garlic.

Cooking
Heat frying pan or wok and add oil. When hot add pork, garlic and spring onions. Stir and turn for 1½ minutes over high heat, and add celery and noodles. When the latter have heated through (in about 1½ minutes), pour the sauce ingredients over them. Stir fry them together over medium heat for 2 minutes. Leave to simmer over low heat for 2½ more minutes and serve.

Serving
Serve in a large bowl or deep sided serving dish. Excellent to consume with rice.

魚類

7. Fish

Empress's Simulation of Crab

(FOR 5-6 PEOPLE)

1 lb. (340-450g.) filleted white fish
7-8 egg whites
1½ tbs. cornflour
1 tbs. warm oil
¼ pint (145 ml.) vegetable oil

for garnish
1-2 egg yolks
2 tsp. minced root ginger
3 tsp. vinegar

for cooking sauce
3 tbs. good chicken stock
1½ tsp. salt
½ tsp. taste powder or MSG (optional)

Preparation
Cut fish into double matchstick sized pieces. Sprinkle with cornflour and mix well. Beat egg whites lightly. Add them to the fish with the warm oil and mix them well together.

Prepare 'cooking sauce' by heating stock with salt and MSG for ¼ minute and put aside.

Cooking
Heat wok and add oil. When hot remove wok from heat for ¼ minute. Pour in the fish/egg white mixture. Turn it around several times, and replace the wok over gentle heat. Continue to turn and stir gently for about 2½ minutes, or until the egg whites set. Drain away all excess oil. Pour the 'cooking sauce' over the contents and continue to turn and stir gently over low heat for 2 minutes.

Serving
Serve on a well heated serving dish. Break 1 or 2 egg yolks over the fish. Finely chop ginger and mix with vinegar, pour it over the top

of the yolks and serve. Good quality soya sauce may also be added for flavour.

Steamed Cabbage Rolls Stuffed with Fish and Crab-Meat

(FOR 6-8 PEOPLE)

6-8 large Chinese cabbage leaves
½ lb. (225g.) filleted fish
½ lb. (225g.) crab-meat
1½ tsp. salt
2 slices ginger
1 egg white
pepper (to taste)
1 tsp. sesame oil

Preparation
Blanch cabbage leaves in boiling water for 1 minute to soften. Drain and dry. Chop fish coarsely and ginger finely. Put them all into a basin together with salt, egg white, pepper (to taste), sesame oil and crab-meat. Mix them together with a fork until fairly consistent.

Open 2 cabbage leaves on a flat board, and put ⅓ to ¼ of the fish/crab-meat into the centre of the leaves and form the stuffing into an elongated strip. Roll the leaves over carefully and firmly into a roll. Trim off the edges at the end, and place it on a heatproof dish. Repeat until all the fish and crab-meat have been used up.

Cooking
Insert the 3-4 cabbage rolls on the heatproof dish into a steamer and steam vigorously for 12-13 minutes.

Serving
Because of the steaming the cabbage rolls should now be firmer. Place them on a chopping board and cut each roll into 4-5 sections. Place them on a serving dish to be eaten hot, accompanied by small dishes of good quality soya sauce and chilli sauce, for use as dips.

Quick-Fried 'Crystal Prawns'

(FOR 5-6 PEOPLE)

1 lb. (450g.) large shrimps or prawns (fresh or frozen)
1 egg white
1 tbs. cornflour
5-6 tbs. vegetable oil
1 tsp. finely chopped ginger
2 tsp. finely chopped onion
³⁄₄ tsp. salt
¹⁄₄ tsp. MSG (optional)
2 tbs. good stock
1 tbs. dry sherry
¹⁄₂ tbs. vinegar

Preparation
Clean and remove the shell and dark vein from the shrimps (if necessary). Beat egg white and blend with cornflour in a bowl. Add shrimps to mix and take on a coating of batter.

Cooking
Heat oil in a hot pan (or wok). When hot remove pan from heat for 10 seconds and add the shrimps. Turn and separate the shrimps in the warm oil, and stir fry them over low heat for 1¹⁄₂ minutes. Remove and put aside. Pour away any excess oil and add ginger, onion, salt, MSG, sherry and stock to the pan to stir fry together with shrimps and the other ingredients for ¹⁄₄ minute. Return prawns to the pan. Turn and toss with other ingredients for ¹⁄₂ minute over high heat. Sprinkle with vinegar.

Serving
Serve hot as soon as cooked.

Three-Tier Crispy Fish

(FOR 6-8 PEOPLE)

³⁄₄ lb. (340g.) white fish (filleted)
6-8 slices white bread
6 slices ham (cooked or uncooked)
1¹⁄₂ tsp. salt
¹⁄₂ tbs. white wine

½ tbs. *cornflour*
1 tbs. *black sesame seeds*

for batter
1 egg
4 tbs. plain flour
1 tbs. cornflour
2 tbs. water

for dips
salt and pepper mix (preferably heated first)
ketchup
soya sauce and chilli sauce mix

Preparation
Cut fish into 12-16 thin slices about 2″ x 1½″. Sprinkle and rub with salt, wine and cornflour. Mix the ingredients for the batter in a bowl into a batter. Cut each piece of ham into 2-3 pieces.

Place slices of bread on a board or tray. Spread the top of each slice with a good layer of batter and rub it in. Place 2-3 pieces of fish on top of each slice of battered bread and press down. In turn spread the top of each piece of fish with batter, and press on top a couple of slices of ham. Spread some batter on top of the ham and sprinkle with sesame seeds.

Cooking
Heat oil in the deep-fryer to about 300°F. If using an ordinary frying pan, use 1 pint of oil. Lower 1 piece of 'open sandwich' at a time into the hot oil, ham/fish side down first, fry for about 2 minutes. Turn it over and fry for just 1 minute on the other side. Remove to drain on absorbent paper.

Serving
Remove the rind from the edge of the bread and cut each slice into 3-4 convenient bite-size pieces. Serve hot, using salt pepper mix, ketchup and soya sauce with chilli sauce as dips.

Triple-Fry of 'Three Sea Flavours' with Chilli and Black Bean Sauce

(FOR 4-5 PEOPLE)

¼-⅓ lb. (115-150g.) large prawns (shelled)
3-4 scallops
3-4 oz. (85-115g.) squid (or breast of chicken)
2 slices root ginger
1-2 cloves garlic
½ medium red sweet pepper
2 spring onions
3-4 tsp. salted black beans
3 tsp. chilli sauce (or 'red-oil')
1 tbs. soya sauce
6 tbs. good stock
¾ tbs. cornflour (blended in 3 tbs. water)
5-6 tbs. vegetable oil
1½ tsp. sesame oil
1 tbs. sherry
1 tsp. salt, pepper (to taste)

Preparation
Cut each prawn in 2-3 sections, scallops into quarters and squid or chicken into similar sized pieces. Sprinkle and rub with salt and pepper (to taste). Soak black beans in warm water for 5 minutes. Drain and chop finely.

Cut ginger into ¼" slices, spring onions into 1" sections, garlic into very thin slices, and red pepper into 1" x ½" pieces.

Cooking
Heat 4 tbs. oil in a frying pan. When very hot add the prawns, scallops and squid (or chicken). Stir fry and turn them quickly over high heat for 1½ minutes. Remove with perforated spoon and put aside.

Pour remaining oil into the pan. Add ginger, garlic and black beans. Stir them together over high heat for ½ minute. Add spring onions and pepper. Stir them together with the other contents of the pan for ½ minute. Add stock and cook together for 1¼ minutes.

Add soya sauce and chilli sauce, stir them quickly with the other contents in the pan until they are all well blended. Return the prawns, scallops and squid (or chicken) to the pan. Stir and turn them for 1 minute still over high heat. Sprinkle them all with blended cornflour, sesame oil and sherry. Turn and stir a few more times and serve.

Serving
Serve on a well heated serving dish, and consume immediately.

Cantonese Ginger and Onion Crab (or Lobster)

(FOR 5 PEOPLE)

3 lb. (1½ kilos) crab or 2½ lb. (1125g.) lobster (live)
4 slices root ginger
4 spring onions
oil for deep frying
¼ pint good chicken stock
1½ tbs. soya sauce
½ tsp. salt
2 tbs. sherry

Preparation
Chop crab or lobster through shell into large bite-size pieces. Shred ginger and cut onions into 1″ sections.

Cooking
Heat oil in the deep-fryer. When hot add the crab or lobster pieces to the hot oil for 3 minutes. Remove and drain.

Add ginger and 2 spring onions and salt and stir in the hot oil in a frying pan (or wok) with lid for 1 minute. Add stock, soya sauce and sherry. When contents re-boil stir a few times. Add all the pieces of crab (or lobster). Turn them around in the stock sauce, and place a lid firmly over the pan. Leave contents to cook over high heat for 3-4 minutes (when liquid should have reduced by ⅓-½). Transfer the crab or lobster to a deep-sided serving dish, pour the contents from the pan into the dish and sprinkle with remaining spring onions; serve.

Sliced Fish in Curry-Flavoured Sauce

(FOR 4-6 PEOPLE, EATEN WITH OTHER DISHES)

1 lb. (450g.) filleted white fish
1 tsp. salt
1 egg white
1 tbs. cornflour
¼ tsp. black pepper
cornflour (for coating)
4-5 Chinese dried mushrooms
oil for deep frying
1½ tbs. peas (fresh or frozen)

for sauce
2 tsp. chopped onion
1 tbs. curry powder
1 tsp. salt
1 tbs. sugar
1 tbs. white wine
1 tbs. tomato purée
6 tbs. good stock
1 tbs. cornflour (blended in 3 tbs. water)

Preparation
Cut fish into 1″ wide and 1½″ long thick pieces. Rub with salt and pepper. Mix egg white with cornflour and add to the fish pieces to coat them evenly. Leave to marinate for ½ hour. Soak mushrooms in warm water for 20 minutes. Remove stems and cut caps in half.

Cooking
Heat oil in a deep-fryer (or heat ¾ pint oil in a medium size frying pan). When a crumb sizzles when dropped into the oil, coat the pieces of fish with additional cornflour provided and lower them into the oil to deep fry until crisp and brown (in about 2-2½ minutes). Remove and drain.
 Pour oil away from the frying pan. Add onion, salt, mushrooms and curry powder. Stir them over medium heat for 1 minute. Add stock, wine, purée and sugar. Stir quickly for ½ minute. Add blended cornflour. Continue to stir until the sauce thickens. Add peas and return the pieces of fried fish to the sauce. Mix well and turn off the heat.

Serving
Serve on a well heated dish, and consume immediately.

Quick-Fry of 'Three Sea-Flavours' in Wine (Sediment Paste) Sauce

(FOR 4-5 PEOPLE)

1/4-1/3 lb. (115-150g.) large prawns (shelled)
4-5 scallops
3-4 oz. (85-115g.) squid (or breast of chicken)
salt and pepper (to taste)
2 slices root ginger
2 cloves garlic
2 spring onions
1/2 medium size red pepper
5 tbs. vegetable oil
1/2 tbs. cornflour (blended in 3 tbs. water)
1 1/2 tbs. wine-sediment paste (blended in with 2 tbs. rice wine; if not available use 3 tbs. white wine)
1 tbs. soya sauce
1 1/2 tsp. sesame oil

Preparation

Cut each prawn into 3 sections, scallops into quarters, and squid or chicken into similar size pieces. Sprinkle and rub with salt and pepper (to taste).

Chop ginger, cut spring onion into 1″ sections, chop garlic coarsely, and cut pepper into 1″ x 1/2″ pieces.

Cooking and serving

Heat 4 tbs. oil in a wok or frying pan. When very hot add the prawns, scallops and squid (or chicken). Stir fry them quickly over high heat for 1 3/4 minutes. Remove with perforated spoon and put aside.

Pour remaining oil into the pan. Add ginger, garlic, spring onions and pepper. Stir fry them quickly over the high heat for 1/2 minute. Add soya sauce, wine-sediment paste mixture (or wine) and blended cornflour. Stir them together. When the mixture starts to boil return the 'seafoods' to the pan to turn and stir in the sauce with the other ingredients for 1 1/2 minutes. Sprinkle with sesame oil and serve.

Crispy-Fried and Braised Whole Fish in Shredded Pork and Mushrooms

(FOR 5-6 PEOPLE)

1 fish (2 lb./1 kilo mullet, sea-bass, trout, etc.)
2 tsp. salt
3-4 tbs. cornflour
1 egg
oil for deep frying

for sauce
4 tbs. light soya sauce
4 spring onions
2 tbs. lard (or oil)
¼ lb. (115g.) lean & fat pork
½ lb. (225g.) mushrooms
5 tbs. good stock
3 tbs. dry sherry
1 tbs. vinegar
4 slices root ginger
3 tsp. sugar
pepper (to taste)

Preparation
After cleaning fish thoroughly, sprinkle and rub with salt and cornflour and wet with beaten egg.

Cut spring onions into 2″ sections and shred pork, mushrooms and ginger. Heat fat or oil in a saucepan. When hot add pork, onions and mushrooms and stir fry over high heat for 2 minutes. Add all the remaining sauce ingredients and bring to boil; reduce heat to low and simmer for 4 minutes.

Cooking
Heat oil in a deep fryer or 2 pints of oil in a large frying pan. When hot (when a crumb will sizzle) lower the fish to fry in it for 4-5 minutes. If fried in a large frying pan, pour away all the oil(or as much as possible). Then pour in all the contents of saucepan and spread them evenly over the length of the fish. Cook gently until the liquid in the pan has been reduced to one third.

Serving
Serve on a large well heated oval dish. Pour the remainder of the reduced sauce from the pan over the fish and garnish with mushrooms, shredded pork and spring onions.

Peking Kuo Ta Fish Omelette

(FOR 4-5 PEOPLE)

½-¾ lb. (225-340g.) filleted flat fish (sole, plaice, etc.)
5-6 eggs
1½ tsp. salt
pepper (to taste)
5-6 tbs. vegetable oil
1½ tsp. sesame oil
3 spring onions
6 tbs. chicken stock
1 tbs. light soya sauce
1 tbs. dry sherry
4 slices ginger
3 cloves garlic

Preparation
Sprinkle fish with salt, pepper and sesame oil, and rub them in. Beat eggs in a basin, and add fish to take on a coating of beaten egg. Chop spring onions, garlic and ginger finely.

Cooking
Heat wok or large frying pan. Add oil; when hot (when a crumb will sizzle), lay the fish in one piece in the hot oil, pour all the beaten egg on top and shake pan to loosen the contents. Cooking over high/medium heat, the egg will begin to set in 3-3½ minutes. Turn the fish omelette over with a fish-slice and leave to fry for a further 2½ minutes.
   Sprinkle the shredded onions, garlic and ginger all around the pan, surrounding the omelette and on top of it. Mix the stock with soya sauce and sherry and pour the mixture over the omelette and into the pan. Leave the contents to simmer for further 4 minutes. Transfer the omelette onto a well heated serving dish.

Serving
Heat the liquid left in the pan momentarily over high heat, pour it over the fish omelette in the serving dish and garnish omelette with the shredded vegetables.

Quick-Fried Diced Fish with Croutons, Ham and Straw-Mushrooms

(FOR 5-6 PEOPLE)

$\frac{1}{2}$-$\frac{3}{4}$ *lb. (225-340g.) fillet of white fish*
1$\frac{1}{2}$ tsp. salt
2 tbs. cornflour
1 egg white
2 slices white bread
4 tbs. green peas (fresh or frozen)
1 can straw mushrooms (or small champignons)
3 tbs. good stock (blended with 2 tsp. cornflour)
1 tbs. light soya sauce
$\frac{1}{2}$ tsp. taste powder (or $\frac{1}{2}$ crumbled chicken stock cube)
1 tbs. dry sherry
1-2 slices root ginger
$\frac{1}{4}$ lb. (115g.) gammon
2 spring onions
oil for deep frying or semi deep frying ($\frac{1}{2}$-1 pint/290-575 ml. oil in frying pan)

Preparation
Cut fish into $\frac{1}{2}$" cubes, sprinkle and rub with salt and cornflour and wet with egg white. Cut gammon into $\frac{1}{3}$" cubes and spring onions into shavings. Shred ginger. Cut bread into same size cubes as the gammon.

Cooking
Heat oil in the deep-fryer (or 1" depth of oil in a frying pan). When hot add the diced cubes of fish to fry for 1$\frac{1}{4}$ minutes and remove to drain. Turn the heat up under the pan of oil for $\frac{1}{4}$ minute.

Add the bread cubes. Deep fry until crispy and golden brown (in about 1$\frac{1}{2}$ minutes). Remove and drain on absorbent paper.

Heat 2 tbs. oil in another frying pan. Add spring onions, ginger and gammon. Stir them for $\frac{1}{2}$ minute. Add mushrooms and peas. Stir them around for further $\frac{1}{4}$ minute. Pour in the soya sauce, sherry, taste powder and blended stock. Add fish cubes and croutons to the pan. Stir and toss all ingredients together for $\frac{3}{4}$ minute over high heat.

Serving
Serve on a well heated dish and eat hot.

Long-Cook (or Baked) Lotus Leaf Wrapped Whole Fish

(FOR 5-6 PEOPLE)

1 whole fish (mullet, sea-bass, trout – about 2½ lb./1¼ kilos)
2 tbs. soya sauce
1 tsp. salt
2 tbs. hoisin sauce
2 tbs. vegetable oil
2 tbs. dry sherry
3 slices root ginger
3 spring onions

for stuffing
2 onions
2 rashers bacon
¼-½ lb. (115-225g.) mushrooms
1½ tbs. lard

2 lotus leaves
1 large sheet tinfoil

Preparation
Clean fish thoroughly. Mix salt, soya sauce, hoisin, oil and sherry. Rub the fish inside and out with the mixture and leave to season for ½ hour. Shred the ginger and spring onions. Add them to the fish.
    Shred the onions and bacon for stuffing. Cut each mushroom into quarters. Stir fry onions, bacon and mushrooms in lard for 1½ minutes then stuff mushrooms with the bacon and onion into the belly of the fish.
    Soak lotus leaves in hot water for 2 minutes to soften. Drain and dry with absorbent paper. Wrap the fish in the leaves, and, to hold the leaf wrapping secure, wrap the sheet of tinfoil over the parcel.

Cooking
The parcel of fish can now either be inserted into a steamer for ¾ hour of vigorous steaming, or into a pre-heated oven at gas mark 6 (200°C; 400°F) to bake for 25 minutes at this temperature and then reduce heat to mark 2 (160°C; 325°F) for a further 25 minutes.

Serving
Serve by bringing the tinfoil-wrapped fish to the table and opening it in front of the diners. The meat of the fish can be picked with chopsticks and stuffings ladled out with spoons onto the diners' own bowls of rice to consume with the latter.

Deep Fried Crispy King Prawns in Breadcrumbs

(FOR 4-5 PEOPLE)

6 large king prawns
2 tsp. salt
1 egg white
pepper (to taste)
½ lb. (225g.) breadcrumbs
oil for deep frying

Preparation
Clean prawns and remove dark vein from the back. Sprinkle and rub with salt and pepper and wet with egg white. Roll the prawns in the breadcrumbs to take on an even coating.

Cooking
Heat the oil until a crumb will sizzle audibly when dropped into it. Lower the prawns one by one into the hot oil. Allow the prawns to fry for 2½ minutes. Remove and drain on absorbent paper.

Serving
Cut the prawns lengthwise into 3-4 long strips and serve. To be eaten hot, using good quality soya sauce, chilli sauce and ketchup as dips.

Kai Lung Steamed Sliced Fish Interleaved with Ham and Broccoli

(FOR 4-6 PEOPLE)

1 lb. (450g.) filleted white fish (plaice, sole, etc.)
½ lb. (225g.) smoked ham
2 tsp. salt and pepper (to taste)
1½ tbs. cornflour
1 egg white
½ lb. (225g.) broccoli
1 tbs. light soya sauce
2 tbs. good stock
¼ tsp. taste powder (optional)
1½ tbs. vegetable oil

Preparation

Cut fish into 2½″ x 1½″ pieces. Sprinkle and rub with salt, pepper, cornflour, ½ tbs. oil and egg white. Mix remaining oil with soya sauce, stock and taste powder (optional).

Cut ham and broccoli into similar size pieces as the fish. Wet and soak them for a few minutes in the oil soya stock mixture.

Cooking

Arrange the fish, ham and broccoli interleaved in a heatproof dish in an interesting pattern. Insert the dish into a steamer to steam vigorously for 8-10 minutes.

Serving

Bring the dish out from the steamer, clouded in steam, and serve on the table. With the red of the ham, white of the fish, and green of the vegetable and the contrast between flavour and texture of all three materials, the dish makes for an appealing presentation on a party table.

Quick-Braised King Prawns in Shells in 'Reduced Sauce'

(FOR 4-6 PEOPLE)

10-12 large king prawns in shells (fresh or frozen)
4 slices root ginger
3 spring onions
2 cloves garlic
4 tbs. vegetable oil

for sauce

2 tbs. soya sauce
1 tbs. hoisin sauce
½ tbs. yellow bean sauce
1 tbs. tomato purée
1 tsp. chilli sauce
3 tbs. good stock
2 tbs. dry sherry
½ tbs. sugar
2 tsp. sesame oil

Preparation

Remove the head and dark vein from the back of prawns (but not the shell) and clean thoroughly. Chop ginger, garlic and spring onions finely.

Mix the sauce ingredients into a cooking sauce.

Cooking

Heat oil in a wok or frying pan. Add onions and ginger and stir around over medium heat for $1/3$ minute. Add the prawns and garlic and turn and stir them in hot, flavoured oil for 1 minute.

Pour in the blended sauce. Stir and turn the prawns in the sauce and leave them to cook in the latter over low-medium heat for about $1\frac{1}{2}$-2 minutes, or until the sauce has been reduced to $\frac{1}{4}$.

Sprinkle the contents with sesame oil and turn them over a couple of times.

Serving

A typical Chinese party dish to serve with wine. The gravy or sauce should be sucked off from prawns and enjoyed before removing the shells from the prawns to get at the meat.

Sweet and Sour Fish

(FOR 4-5 PEOPLE)

1 lb. (450g.) filleted fish (plaice, sole, cod, haddock, etc.)
1½ tsp. salt
2 tbs. cornflour
2 tbs. self-raising flour
1 egg
oil for deep frying (or semi deep frying)

for sauce
2 slices pineapple
2-3 tbs. pineapple syrup
2 tbs. tomato purée
1 tbs. soya sauce
3 tbs. vinegar
2 lbs. sugar
1-2 tbs. orange juice
1½ tbs. cornflour (blended in 3 tbs. water)

Preparation

Cut fish into 1½" x 1" pieces. Rub with salt. Mix cornflour and self-raising flour with beaten egg to make a batter. Add the batter to the fish in a basin.

Cut each slice of pineapple into a dozen regular pieces. Mix pineapple syrup with tomato purée, soya sauce, vinegar, sugar, orange juice and blended cornflour until well mixed.

Cooking
Heat oil in a deep fryer, or 1½ pints/1 litre of oil in a deep frying pan. When a crumb will sizzle when dropped into the hot oil, add the battered fish piece by piece to deep fry for 2½-3 minutes. Remove and drain.

In a separate frying pan heat 2 tbs. oil. When hot add the pineapple pieces, stir them around for ½ minute, and then pour in the blended ingredients of the 'sweet and sour sauce'. Stir them around so that the heating will be even. When the sauce thickens and becomes translucent add the fish pieces to the sauce, turn them around a few times, and leave to cook in the sauce for ½-¾ minute.

Serving
Serve them on a well heated deep-sided dish and eat hot.

Quick-Fried Prawns in Fu-Yung 'Bed of Jade'

(FOR 4-5 PEOPLE)

¾ lb. (340g.) large shelled prawns
1½ tsp. salt
pepper (to taste)
1 tsp. ground ginger
1½ tbs. cornflour
1 egg whites
oil for semi deep frying

for Fu-Yung 'bed of Jade'
3 egg whites
1½ tsp. salt
pepper (to taste)
6-7 tbs. minced spinach
1½ tbs. lard (melted)
½ tsp. taste powder (optional)

Preparation
Sprinkle and rub the prawns with salt, ginger and pepper. Dust with cornflour and wet with egg white. Beat 3 egg whites and mix with spinach, lard, salt, pepper and taste powder.

Cooking
Heat oil for semi deep frying (1½ pints/1 litre in a deep frying pan). When a crumb sizzles when dropped into it, add the prawns to deep fry for 1¼ minutes. Remove and drain. Heat 4 tbs. oil in a separate frying pan. When hot add the spinach/Fu-Yung mixture. Stir and turn them around until the mixture firms (in about 2 minutes). Add the prawns to stir and turn with the other ingredients for ¾ minute. Sprinkle with sesame oil and serve.

Serving
Serve in a well heated serving dish for consumption with rice or as starter to consume with wine.

麵飯

8. Rice and Noodles

Rice is an important staple food of China and an indispensable complement to all rich savoury dishes during normal meals (except for banquets when no rice is served). I shall risk repeating myself in describing how it can be cooked since even many restaurants these days are resorting to using the electric rice-cooker with consequent loss of the habit of cooking rice the easy 'normal way'.

Boiled Rice

(FOR 4-6 PEOPLE)

¾ pint (430 ml.) rice
1 pint (575 ml.) water (or: 2 measures of rice to 3 of water)

Preparation and cooking
Wash and rinse rice a couple of times until the water is clear. Put it in a saucepan with a tight-fitting cover. Add 1 pint of water. Turn on the heat. When contents boil reduce the heat and leave rice to simmer gently for 8-10 minutes. Turn heat off and leave rice to stand and cook in the remainder of the heat for another 10 minutes, when the rice should be well cooked and flaky.

Vegetable Rice

(FOR 4-6 PEOPLE)

'Vegetable rice' is very much a dish-of-the-people in Shanghai and the region south of the Yangtze. It simply consists of cooking vegetables together with rice. The procedure is usually to stir fry the vegetable or vegetables first at the bottom of a saucepan with a little salt, and then add half-cooked rice on top and leave the contents to simmer gently for a further 5-6 minutes. Then leave them to stand in the remainder of the heat to cook for another 5-6 minutes.

1¼ lb. (565g.) semi-cooked rice (boiled for 5-6 minutes and still a little watery)
½ lb. (225g.) spring cabbage
3-4 young carrots
3 tbs. vegetable oil (or lard)
2 tsp. salt

Preparation and cooking
Add 2 cups of rice to 3 cups of water in a saucepan. Bring to boil and simmer for 5-6 minutes. Clean cabbage and cut into 2″-3″ size pieces; clean and cut carrots into 2″ sections. Heat oil in a saucepan. Add the vegetables, sprinkle with salt and stir fry them together for 3 minutes. Pour the semi-cooked rice on top of the vegetables. Reduce heat to low and leave contents to simmer for 5 minutes. Turn off the heat and allow the contents to stand and cook in the remainder of the heat for the next 5-6 minutes.

As vegetables are already provided in the 'bulk food' being cooked together with rice, 'vegetable rice' can be served as a complete meal with just one meat dish.

Fried Rice

'Fried rice' differs from the two preceding 'rice' dishes in that it is prepared with cooked rice. It probably came about in the Chinese kitchen in that there was always a collection of chopped up left-overs which could be utilized to advantage by combining them with rice. 'Fried rice' is never served at a banquet and is seldom served in a restaurant in China since on these occasions there is a plentiful provision of delicious savoury dishes, which require to be served with plain bland food — boiled rice. On the other hand, in home-cooking when there is not a profusion of meaty-savoury dishes on the table, fried rice is often served. Here in the West 'fried rice' is often called for as what the average westerner appreciates about Chinese food is its savouriness and fried rice is more savoury than plain boiled rice.

Egg Fried Rice

(FOR 4-5 PEOPLE)

'Egg fried rice' is the simplest and plainest of the fried rice dishes. It simply consists of chopping one medium or large onion coarsely and stir frying it in 3-4 tbs. of oil for 1½-2 minutes. Add a couple of beaten eggs with 2 tsp. salt. Scramble the eggs until they set and then add ¾-1 lb. (340-450g.) cooked rice. Turn them together until evenly mixed. The appeal of 'egg fried rice' lies in its light yellow colour and its onion flavour which makes it an useful accompaniment to other savoury dishes. No soya sauce should be added to 'egg fried rice'.

Vegetable Fried Rice

(FOR 4-5 PEOPLE)

Any number of vegetables may be chopped and added to prepare a 'vegetable fried rice'. The ones most frequently included are: onion, peas, tomato, peppers, mushrooms, cucumber, and a small amount of pickles (gherkins may be used), and a couple of tsp. of finely chopped root ginger. Because of the variety of vegetables used only 2-3 tbs. of each are required. They only require to be stir fried together for 2-3 minutes in a reasonable amount of oil (4-5 tbs.) or fat with 2 tsp. salt, before cooked rice (¾ lb./340g.) is added to mix and stir fry together with them. When the ingredients are well mixed and heated through in 2½-3 minutes, a tbs. or two of soya sauce may be sprinkled over them to provide added flavour. This added flavouring with soya sauce is permissible because 'fried rice' is often served at home in China when there is not a great deal of meat or other savoury food available in the kitchen. When vegetables are so quickly cooked they retain a good deal of their own fresh natural flavour. It is this apparent freshness of flavour which gives the dish its appeal.

Yangchow Special Fried Rice

(FOR 4-5 PEOPLE)

Why Yangchow? Well, Yangchow is a river port on the lower Yangtze, where fresh-water produce is plentiful. It is also a town well known for its cuisine. Hence Yangchow 'special fried rice' is one stage richer and more elaborate than ordinary fried rice: it should contain pork (or ham), and fresh-water shrimps.

It can be prepared simply by adding 3-4 oz. (85-115g.) of pork and the same amount of shrimps to the previous recipe of 'vegetable fried rice'. The pork should be cut into small $\frac{1}{2}$-$\frac{1}{4}$ sugar-lump-size cubes and added with the shrimps into the stir frying before rice is added. With all the ingredients and materials freshly cooked, the Yangchow special fried rice can be a satisfying and delectable dish even if accompanied by nothing else except for a bowl of soup. It should not only be abounding with natural flavour; it should also be richly savoury because of the added pork and shrimps.

The Hainan 'Chicken Rice'

(FOR 4-6 PEOPLE)

Hainan is China's southernmost island. It is about the size of Ireland and the one place in China which is distinctly tropical in climate. Being an unsophisticated region which is only recently being developed, this 'chicken rice' is one of the better known of its dishes.

1 medium size chicken (3½ lb./1¾ kilo)
3 slices root ginger
3 tsp. salt
2 chicken stock cubes
¾ lb. (340g.) broccoli or fresh spring cabbage (greens)
¼ lb. (115g.) green peas
2 medium onions
1 lb. (450g.) rice

Preparation
Wash, rinse and boil rice in an equal amount (volume) of water for 5-6 minutes and leave to stand until all the water is absorbed into the rice. Chop chicken through skin and bone into large 2"-3" bite-size pieces. Cut broccoli (or spring greens) into similar size pieces and onion into thin slices.

Cooking
Heat chicken in a large casserole in 2½ pints (1½ litres) of water, with ginger, onion and salt. When the contents boil, reduce heat to a simmer and leave to cook gently for 50 minutes. Remove the chicken and put aside and discard the ginger. Skim away some of the excess fat. Add the stock cubes, broccoli (or spring greens), onions and peas to the stock. Bring contents to boil and stir them around a few times (until all the stock cubes have dissolved).

Finally add all the rice to the stock and leave to cook gently for 10-12 minutes until all the stock has been absorbed.

Serving
Arrange the chicken pieces on top of the rice and vegetables; close the top of the casserole with a lid to allow the chicken to heat through in 4-5 minutes over the lowest heat. Serve by placing the casserole at the centre of the dining table for the diners to help themselves with spoonfuls of the rice and vegetables. The chicken pieces should be consumed by dipping them into 3-4 dishfuls of good quality soya sauce to which are added varying quantities of chopped garlic, spring onions and small amounts of sesame oil.

A slightly more elaborate version of this 'chicken rice' would have 2-3 lengths of Chinese 'salami sausages' cut into 1"-2" sections which are tucked into the hot rice to steam with the chicken pieces when the latter are replaced on top of the rice for the final heat-up.

Noodles

We usually use fresh hand-drawn noodles in the restaurant. If these are not available you can use most Chinese noodles or even spaghetti.

Plain Stir Fried Noodles with Bean Sprouts and Mushrooms

(FOR 3-4 PEOPLE)

¾-1 lb. (340-450g.) Chinese egg-noodles
4-5 medium Chinese dried mushrooms
½ lb. (225g.) bean sprouts
1 tsp. salt
2 tbs. soya sauce
1 tbs. dried shrimps
3 tbs. good stock
3 tbs. vegetable oil
1 tbs. lard
2 spring onions
1½ tsp. sesame oil

Preparation
Soak mushrooms and dried shrimps in hot water for ½ hour. Drain and chop shrimps into small pieces and shred caps of mushrooms (discarding mushroom stems). Plunge noodles into boiling water and boil for 5-6 minutes, then drain. Rinse under running water to keep separate. Cut spring onions into 1" sections (keep the green and white parts apart).

Cooking
Heat oil in a large frying pan. When hot add the mushrooms, shrimps and the white parts of the spring onions. Stir them together over medium heat for 1½ minutes. Add lard, and when it has melted add the stock, salt and bean sprouts. Stir them all together for another 1½ minutes. Finally add the noodles, and spread them to mix with the other ingredients. Sprinkle contents evenly with soya sauce. Stir and turn them around for 2 minutes and see that the noodles are well heated through.

Serving
Sprinkle the noodles with the green parts of the spring onions and sesame oil. Serve on a well heated dish for the diners to help themselves.

Vegetarian Chow Mein (Chow Mein means stir fried noodles)

(FOR 3-4 PEOPLE)

Repeat the previous recipe, eliminating the lard and shrimps, and use an extra 1½ tbs. of oil in the second phase of the stir frying, when 2-3 different types of additional vegetables (in quantities of 3 oz. (85g.) each) such as shredded french beans, snow peas, broccoli, asparagus, etc, are added to the pan along with ½ tbs. minced root ginger, 1½ tbs. minced Szechuan Ja Chai pickles, 1½ tsp. salt, and 5-6 tbs. water. Half boil and half stir fry them together over high heat for 3-4 minutes when the bean sprouts and noodles are added. Allow the noodles to heat through thoroughly. Sprinkle the noodles with soya sauce and sesame oil and serve (either in individual bowls or in a large well-heated communal bowl from which the diners can help themselves).

'Special Chow Mein' or Stir Fried Noodles with Shredded Meat and Shrimps

(FOR 3-4 PEOPLE)

Repeat recipe 1 or 2 and add ¼-⅓ lb. (115-150g.) shredded pork or chicken breast meat into the first phase of the stir frying, together with the mushrooms and dried shrimps. When they have been stir fried together for 3 minutes over the high heat, add the additional shredded vegetables to stir fry together with other ingredients for a further 2½ minutes with an extra 2 tbs. oil. Finally the bean sprouts and noodles are added and sprinkled with soya sauce.

3-4 tbs. of fresh prawns may be added; chop each prawn into 3-4 pieces and stir fry with 2 tsp. chopped garlic and the remaining ½ of the green spring onions in 2 tbs. oil and 1 tbs. soya sauce for use to garnish the noodles when they are served.

Cantonese Stir Fried Ho-Feng, Flat Rice-Flour Noodles with Sliced Beef in Black Bean Sauce

(FOR 3 PEOPLE)

¾ lb. (340g.) broad ho-feng noodles
1 lb. (450g.) lean beef
1 tsp. salt
pepper to taste
½ tbs. finely chopped root ginger
2 tbs. salted black beans
5 tbs. vegetable oil
2 tsp. chilli sauce
1½ tbs. soya sauce
1 tbs. cornflour (blended in 4-5 tbs. good stock)
1½ tbs. oyster sauce
1 red pepper

Preparation
Soak black beans in hot water for 10 minutes and chop finely. Cut pepper into 2″ x 2″ pieces, and beef into similar size thin pieces. Sprinkle and rub beef with salt, pepper and ½ tbs. oil.

Preparation
Parboil noodles for 7-8 minutes and drain.

Cooking and serving
Heat oil in a frying pan. Add black beans and chopped ginger. Stir them together over high heat for 1½ minutes. Add beef pepper, soya sauce, oyster sauce and chilli sauce and continue to stir fry over high heat for 2½ minutes. Pour in the blended cornflour. Turn it with other ingredients until the sauce thickens. Remove ½ the quantity of the ingredients from the pan. Add the noodles to turn and cook in the sauce with the other ingredients for 3 minutes. Transfer to a serving dish. Return the balance of the ingredients and sauce to the pan with additional 1 tbs. each of oil, soya sauce, oyster sauce and stock (or sherry). Bring to quick boil, and pour the contents over the noodles as garnish and sauce and serve.

Fukien Seafood Noodles

(FOR 4 PEOPLE)

Being a coastal province, Fukien cooking often incorporates a variety of seafoods into noodles. The noodles used are normally rice-flour noodles, which when used are frequently boiled for no more than 2-3 minutes and then immediately drained (they can then be used either for stir frying or in soups). Being so briefly boiled they retain a very firm texture. One of the more unusual seafoods which when available (mostly in the winter) is incorporated into the cooking of noodles is oysters, which impart exceptional savouriness to the noodles. (In this recipe oysters are optional; mussels can be substituted or both can be omitted.)

1 packet (about 1 lb./450g.) rice-flour noodles
2 tsp. salt
2½ tbs. dried shrimps
¼ lb. (115g.) Chinese dried mushrooms
3 slices root ginger
4 rashers bacon
3 stalks young leeks
3-4 oz. (85-115g.) crab-meat (cooked or uncooked)
5 tbs. vegetable oil
8-9 tbs. good stock
1 chicken stock cube
10 medium oysters (optional; or mussels can be substituted)
1½ tbs. lard
2 spring onions
1 tbs. sherry
1 tbs. soya sauce

Preparation
Blanch noodles in boiling water for 2 minutes. Drain and rinse under running water. Soak shrimps and mushrooms in water for 30 minutes. Drain and cut mushroom caps into matchstick shreds (after removing and discarding stems). Chop shrimps coarsely. Shred bacon and ginger. Cut leeks and spring onions into ¼" sections. Crush and chop garlic coarsely. Dip oysters or mussels for ½ minute in boiling water, and remove from shells. Dissolve stock cube by heating it briefly in the stock.

Cooking
Heat 3 tbs. oil in a large frying pan or saucepan (or wok). When hot add the shrimps, bacon, mushrooms and ginger, and stir fry them for 3 minutes over medium heat. Add the noodles to turn and mix with the other ingredients until they have heated through. Heat

balance of oil in a small frying pan.

Add leeks, garlic and crab-meat, sprinkle them with salt, and stir fry them together over medium heat for 2 minutes. Pour in half the stock and continue to stir fry them together 2 more minutes. Pour them evenly over the noodles in the first pan. Turn and mix them evenly with the noodles. Put lard into the empty small frying pan. Heat until it dissolves. Add the oysters, spring onions. Stir them over medium heat for 1/4 minute. Pour in the stock, soya sauce and sherry, heat and stir for one more minute. Turn and mix all the ingredients together evenly over medium heat.

Serving
Transfer the noodles (with all the sauce and ingredients mixed in) to a large well heated serving bowl or dish. Pour the remainder of the contents in the frying pan evenly over the top of the noodles. A dish of exceptional savouriness.

The Szechuan Dan Dan Noodles

(FOR 4-5 PEOPLE)

1 lb. (450g.) noodles (rice-stick or hand-drawn)
1 pint (575 ml.) good stock
2 tsp. salt
1/2 tsp. flavour powder
1 1/2 tbs. sesame paste

for sauce
1/2 lb. (225g.) minced pork
5-6 medium Chinese dried mushrooms
2 tbs. dried shrimps
2 tbs. chopped Szechuan Jai Chai pickles
3 tsp. minced root ginger
2 spring onions
1/2 tsp. salt
2 tsp. yellow bean paste
1 1/2 tbs. soya sauce
3 tsp. chilli sauce
2 red dried chilli peppers
3 tbs. vegetable oil
1/4 pint (145 ml.) good stock (blended with 1 tbs. cornflour)

Preparation

Boil noodles for 3-4 minutes and drain. Rinse under running water. Soak mushrooms for 20 minutes in hot water. Drain, remove stems and chop caps into small pieces. Prepare dry shrimps similarly. Chop pepper and spring onions into small pieces (discard pips).

Cooking

Heat stock in saucepan. Add salt, flavour powder, sesame paste and noodles, bring to boil and simmer for 1 minute.

Heat wok and add oil. When hot add first of all mushrooms, shrimps, chilli and ginger. Stir them together over high heat for 1½ minutes. Add pork to mix with the other ingredients and stir and turn over high heat for 2 minutes. Add salt, yellow bean paste, pickle, soya sauce, chilli sauce and onions. Continue to stir and turn for a further 3 minutes. Pour in the stock (blended with cornflour). Stir and bring to boil and leave to simmer gently for 5 minutes.

Serving

Divide the noodles and stock into 4-5 serving bowls. Pour a proportion of the prepared sauce over each bowl of noodles and serve. This is one of those spicy Chinese 'semi-soup' noodle dishes.

The Peking Cha Chiang Mein Noodles

(FOR 3-4 PEOPLE)

1 lb. (450g.) hand-drawn noodles
½-¾ lb. (225-340g.) minced meat (other meat can also be used)
½ tsp. salt
3 tbs. vegetable oil
3-4 tbs. water or stock
1-2 slices root ginger
1½ tbs. cornflour (blended in 3-4 tbs. water)
6" section of medium cucumber
1 tbs. soya sauce
1½ tbs. yellow bean sauce
1 clove garlic
1 medium onion
3-4 spring onions

Preparation
Chop onion, ginger and garlic coarsely. Clean and cut spring onions into 2″-3″ sections, and cucumber into large matchstick strips. Parboil the noodles in boiling water for 3 minutes and drain carefully.

Cooking
Heat oil in a frying pan or wok. When hot add onion and ginger and stir fry for 1 minute. Add garlic and stir fry together for ½ minute. Add the minced pork to mix and stir with the garlic, onion and ginger in the hot oil for 2 minutes. Add salt, yellow bean sauce and soya sauce. Leave to cook over medium heat for 2-3 minutes. Stir and mix and bring to boil. Add water or stock, stir and turn and leave to cook for a further 3-4 minutes. Pour in the blended cornflour to mix with the contents in the pan. Once the 'meat sauce' is thickened it is ready for use.

Serving
Place the parboiled noodles in a large serving bowl. Pour the meat sauce over the centre of the noodles, and arrange the shredded cucumber and spring onion sections round the sides. The noodles and ingredients are tossed together at the table, before dividing up into individual portions for the assembled diners. For greater bulk and a higher proportion of vegetables ¼-½ lb. (115-225g.) of bean sprouts may be lightly parboiled and added to the dish and tossed with the noodles and other ingredients. Other flavouring ingredients (including a small amount of vinegar) may be added according to taste.

蔬菜

9. Vegetables

Quick-Fried Mange Touts with Bean Sprouts

(FOR 4-5 PEOPLE WITH OTHER DISHES)

¾ lb. (340g.) mange touts
¾ lb. (340g.) bean sprouts
4 tbs. vegetable oil
1½ tsp. salt
1-2 oz. (25-55g.) piece Szechuan Ja Chai pickle
2 tsp. sesame oil
1 tbs. soya sauce

Preparation
Cut mange touts into shreds. Cut pickle into similar shreds.

Cooking
Heat oil in a wok. Add Ja Chai pickle and mange touts. Stir fry over high heat for 1½ minutes. Add bean sprouts, sprinkle with salt, soya sauce and 3 tbs. water. Continue to stir fry over high heat for 2½ minutes.
　Sprinkle contents with sesame oil and serve.

Serving
Serve and consume immediately. Here heat is a part of flavour.

Coral Cabbage

(FOR 5-6 PEOPLE WITH RICE AND OTHER DISHES)

This is a vegetarian dish which involves the use of 'red bean curd cheese' as a flavouring, and the quality of the dish becomes more apparent when the vegetable is consumed in quantity. (In contrast to stir-fried vegetables, which are often only consumed as a supplement to meat dishes, here the vegetable is eaten with rice, almost as a 'bulk food'.)

2½-3 lb. (1¼-1½ kilos) Chinese cabbage
2½ tbs. red bean curd 'cheese' (and sauce)
2½ tbs. tomato purée
1 tbs. light soya sauce
salt and pepper (to taste)
4 tbs. vegetable oil
1-2 tbs. lard (or butter)
1½ tbs. dried shrimps (soaked and chopped) (optional)
1-2 tbs. 'winter pickle' (optional)
1 cup good stock (or water, if vegetarian)

Preparation
Cut or tear cabbage into 2-3″ length large pieces. Blend the 'cheese' with purée and soya sauce.

Cooking
Heat oil in a large pan or wok. When hot add shrimps and pickle. Turn them in the oil a few times. Add all the cabbage, and sprinkle it with salt and pepper. Turn the cabbage in the hot oil for a couple of minutes, until it is well coated with oil. Pour the 'cheese'/purée/soya mixture evenly over the vegetable. Turn the cabbage until it is well covered with the red sauce. Transfer the contents into a casserole. Top with the lard. Pour stock over contents. Put the casserole into a pre-heated oven at 175°C (gas mark 3; 350°F) for 30-35 minutes.

Serving
Serve by bringing the casserole to the table: a boon to consume with rice.

The 'Buddhist's Delight' (or the Monk's mixed vegetables)

(FOR 6-8 PEOPLE)

1 cake bean curd
vegetable oil for deep frying

dried vegetables and other items
1-2 oz. (25-55g.) Chinese 'hair seaweeds'
2-3 tiger lily stems (called 'golden needles')

1½ oz. (40g.) 'wood ears'
2 oz. (55g.) pea-starch noodles
¼-½ lb. (115-225g.) broccoli
¼-½ lb. (115-225g.) Chinese cabbage
2 young carrots
2-3 oz. (55-85g.) bamboo shoots
¼ lb. (115g.) aubergine
/₄ lb. (115g.) celery
1 cake bean curd
1½ tbs. soya paste
2 tbs. soya sauce
1½ tbs. oyster sauce
1 pint good stock
½ tsp. flavour powder (or 1 chicken stock cube)
2 tbs. dry sherry
2 tsp. sesame oil

Preparation
Soak 'seaweeds', tiger lily stems, wood ears and pea-starch noodles separately in water for 10 minutes and drain. Cut bean curd into 8 pieces. Deep fry bean curd for 4 minutes and drain. Cut broccoli, carrots, bamboo shoots and aubergine into bite-size pieces, deep fry for 3 minutes and drain. Cut cabbage into 1½" slices, and celery into 1½" sections.

Cooking
Heat 5 tbs. oil in a large casserole. When hot add all the dried, soaked and drained vegetables, as well as the fresh vegetables. Turn them in the oil. Sprinkle with soya sauce, soya paste and oyster sauce; continue to turn, and finally add bean curd, stock, stock cube and transparent pea-starch noodles. Stir, turn and mix all the ingredients together. When they come to the boil, reduce heat to low and allow the contents to simmer gently for 25 minutes. Sprinkle the top with sherry and sesame oil.

Serving
Serve by bringing the casserole to the table; the diners can help themselves. This is a large dish, which is suitable for consumption with an enormous amount of rice.

Clear-Simmered Marrow

(FOR 5-6 PEOPLE WITH OTHER DISHES)

2½ lb.(1-1¼ kilos) marrow
1½ tsp. salt
pepper (to taste)
2 tbs. light coloured soya sauce
3-4 tbs. vegetable oil
1¼ pints good stock
1 chicken stock cube
1½ tbs. dried shrimps
2-3 oz. (55-85g.) transparent pea-starch noodles
2 tsp. sesame oil

Preparation
Scrape or peel marrow; cut into 3" x 2" (thick) pieces. Soak dried shrimps in water for 10 minutes and drain. Soak noodles in water for 5 minutes; cut with scissors into shorter lengths and drain.

Cooking
Heat oil in a saucepan (or casserole). Add the marrow, sprinkle with salt and pepper, and turn it in the oil gently for 2-3 minutes. Add the shrimps and pour in the stock. Bring the contents to the boil. Add noodles, soya sauce and stock cube. When contents re-boil, reduce heat to low and allow them to simmer gently for 25 minutes. Sprinkle with sesame oil.

Serving
As this is a large 'semi-soup' dish it should be served in a large bowl, or in the casserole in which it is cooked. It is a simple homely dish which goes well with quantities of rice.

Clear Hot-Simmered Chinese Cabbage

(FOR 5-6 PEOPLE)

1 medium Chinese cabbage (about 3½ lb./1¾ kilos)
1¼ pints (720 ml.) good stock
2 tbs. dried shrimps
1 chicken stock cube

2 tsp. salt
pepper (to taste)
2-3 red chilli peppers
4 tbs. vegetable oil
1½ tbs. lard

Preparation
Cut cabbage into 1½" slices. Shred chilli peppers, discarding pips. Soak shrimps for 10 minutes and drain.

Cooking
Heat oil in a casserole. When hot add shrimps and chilli. Stir fry them for 1½ minutes. Add the cabbage, sprinkle it with salt and pepper and turn it with the oil, shrimps and chilli. Pour in the stock and add the stock cube (crumbled). Bring contents to boil.

Reduce heat to low, and simmer the contents for the next 20 minutes. Add the lard and continue to simmer for a further 10 minutes.

Serving
Serve by bringing the casserole to the table; the diners can help themselves from it.

Ratatouille Chinoise

(FOR 6-7 PEOPLE)

2 medium onions
6 medium size tomatoes
3 medium courgettes
3 small aubergines
1 each medium red and green peppers
2 small chilli peppers
5-6 tbs. vegetable oil
1 tsp. salt
pepper (to taste)
1½ tbs. black beans
½ tbs. yellow bean sauce
1½ tbs. hoisin sauce
1½ tbs. soya sauce
3 tsp. red bean curd 'cheese'
¼ pint (145 ml.) good stock
1 chicken stock cube

4-6 tbs. red wine
3 tsp. sugar
3 tsp. wine vinegar
2 tsp. sesame oil
2 spring onions

Preparation

Cut onions into thin slices, and tomatoes into quarters or slices. Cut courgettes and aubergines into ¾″ wedge shaped pieces (including skin) and peppers into ½″ x 1″ length strips; chop chilli peppers coarsely. Shred spring onions into ¼″ shavings. Soak black beans in water for 10 minutes. Drain and chop coarsely.

Cooking

Heat oil in a saucepan or frying pan. When hot add tomatoes, courgettes, aubergines, peppers, onions, chilli peppers and black beans. Turn them in the oil and sprinkle them with salt and pepper. Continue to stir fry for 3 minutes. Add all the sauces and 'cheese'. Bring contents to boil. Reduce heat to low and allow the contents to simmer gently for 9-10 minutes. Add stock, and sprinkle it with crumbled stock cube. Add wine and sugar. Continue to cook and stir gently for 10 minutes. Add vinegar and sprinkle contents with sesame oil and spring onion shavings.

Serving

Serve either by dividing into small individual bowls or in a large serving bowl for the diners to help themselves; consume as accompaniment to rice, with which it blends admirably.

Quick-Braised Courgettes in Oyster Sauce

(FOR 4 PEOPLE)

1 lb. (450g.) courgettes
¼ pint (145ml.) vegetable oil
1 tsp. salt
2 cloves garlic

for sauce
1½ tbs. soya sauce

2 tbs. oyster sauce
1 tbs. sherry
3 tbs. good stock
1½ tsp. sugar

Preparation
Cut each courgette into ½″ sections. Crush and chop garlic coarsely.

Cooking
Heat oil in a frying pan. When hot (a crumb will sizzle when dropped into it), add courgettes. Give them 'a turn in the oil' for 1½ minutes. Drain away the oil, and sprinkle the vegetable with salt and garlic. Turn around a few times, and add all the sauce ingredients. Turn them all together for 1 minute. Reduce heat to low, and leave to cook gently under cover for 1½ minutes.

Serving
Serve on a well heated serving dish to accompany rice and complement the meat dishes.

Quick-Fried Mange Touts or Snow Peas

(FOR 4 PEOPLE WITH OTHER DISHES)

1 lb. (450g.) mange touts
2 cloves garlic
2 tbs. good stock
1 tbs. soya sauce
1 tbs. oyster sauce
½ tsp. salt
¼ pint vegetable oil

Preparation
Clean, trim and top-and-tail the mange touts. Chop garlic finely.

Cooking and serving
Heat oil in a frying pan. When hot (a crumb will sizzle when dropped into it) add all the mange touts. Stir and turn them over to give them a coating of oil for 1½ minutes. Reduce heat to low and continue to fry gently for 1½ minutes. Drain away all excess oil, sprinkle vegetable with salt and garlic. Turn and stir it around for

½ minute. Add soya sauce, stock and oyster sauce.

Turn and mix all the ingredients well together. Leave to cook for one further minute and serve.

Quick-Fried Bean Sprouts with Transparent Pea-Starch Noodles

(FOR 4-5 PEOPLE WITH OTHER DISHES)

1 lb. (450g.) bean sprouts
3 spring onions
2 cloves garlic
2 slices ginger
2 tsp. salt
4-5 oz. (115-140g.) transparent pea-starch noodles
4 tbs. vegetable oil
2 tsp. sesame oil
¼ tsp. freshly ground pepper
3-4 tbs. lard (or butter)
3-4 tbs. stock

for flavouring noodles
4 Chinese dried mushrooms
1½ tbs. dried shrimps
¼ pint hot water
1½ tbs. soya sauce
1 tbs. vinegar

Preparation
Chop ginger and garlic finely. Cut spring onions into 1″ sections.

Soak mushrooms and dried shrimps in hot water for ½ hour. Remove stems of the mushrooms and shred caps. Chop shrimps coarsely. Return both the mushrooms and shrimps to the water in which they had been soaked.

Soak noodles in warm or hot water for 5 minutes. Drain and cut them to shorter lengths with a pair of scissors. Add noodles to the bowl containing the mushrooms and dried shrimps. Add soya sauce and vinegar. Turn and mix the contents well together, until the noodles have soaked up all the flavour and the liquid.

Cooking
Heat oil in a large frying pan. When hot add garlic and ginger. Sprinkle with salt, and half the spring onions. Stir them around a

few times. Pour in the noodles with the shrimps and mushrooms. Allow the contents to come to the boil, reduce heat to low and allow contents to simmer gently for 2 minutes. Add stock, lard and bean sprouts. Stir and turn and mix well with the other ingredients to simmer gently for 2 minutes. Sprinkle contents with sesame oil, vinegar and pepper. Turn and stir them around once more.

Serving
Serve to supplement meat or poultry dishes, to be consumed with the rice for which it is a great complement. The savouriness of the noodles provides an excellent contrast to the fresh crunchiness of the bean sprouts.

Braised Aubergine

(FOR 4-6 PEOPLE WITH OTHER DISHES)

3-4 aubergines
3 slices ginger (chopped)
2 cloves garlic (chopped)
1 tbs. hot Szechuan Tou Pan bean paste
2 tbs. soya sauce
1 tbs. vinegar
1 tbs. sugar
½ tbs. salt
6 tbs. good stock
½ tsp. sesame oil
6 tbs. oil
3 spring onions (chopped)

Preparation
Choose firm purple aubergines, remove stalks and, without peeling, cut slantwise into 2″ x 1″ pieces.

Cooking
Heat oil in frying pan until very hot, put aubergines in and turn heat to low; stir fry until they're soft (about 5 minutes). Press aubergines to squeeze out any excess oil. Remove aubergines from pan and set aside.

Put chopped garlic and ginger into the frying pan with hot bean paste, stir them together a few times. Add soya sauce, sugar, salt and stock and bring contents to the boil. Add aubergines, and cook for 2½ minutes until the sauce is reduced to ¼.

Add vinegar and sesame oil, and continue to stir until heated through. Sprinkle with chopped spring onions, mix carefully and serve hot.

Quick-Fried French Beans with Dried Shrimps, Garlic, Onion and Pickles

(FOR 4-6 PEOPLE WITH OTHER DISHES)

1½ lb. (675g.) french beans
2-3 oz. (55-85g.) minced meat (pork)
2 tbs. Chinese dried shrimps
2 tbs. chopped spring onions
1 tbs. chopped Szechuan Ja Chai pickle
3 tbs. good stock
3 tsp. chopped garlic (2 cloves)
1½ tbs. lard
oil for deep frying (if using a frying pan 1 pint/575 ml. oil is needed)

for flavouring
1 tbs. soya sauce
½ tbs. sugar
2 tsp. vinegar
2 tsp. salt
1 tsp. sesame oil
3 tbs. water

Preparation
Top-and-tail, and clean the French beans thoroughly. After soaking in water for 20 minutes, chop the dried shrimps finely. Wash and rinse the pickle and also chop finely.

Cooking and serving
Heat oil in a deep fryer until a crumb will sizzle when dropped into it. Add the beans and turn them in the hot oil for 2 minutes. Remove the beans with perforated spoon and put aside. Pour away the oil for other uses.

Add lard to the remainder of oil in the pan. Add garlic, stir a few times, follow with the minced pork, chopped shrimps, stock and pickles. Stir them all together for 2 minutes, then add soya sauce, sugar, salt, water. Add all the beans and turn quickly with all the other ingredients.

Turn and stir until the liquid in the pan has nearly all evaporated. Sprinkle the contents with sesame oil, vinegar and chopped spring onions. Turn and stir once more, and serve.

Quick-Braised Broad Beans with Mushrooms

(FOR 4-5 PEOPLE WITH OTHER DISHES)

½-¾ lb. (225-340g.) broad beans (fresh or frozen)
¼ lb. (115g.) small firm button mushrooms
6-8 Chinese dried mushrooms
½ pint (290ml.) vegetable oil

for sauce
2 tbs. soya sauce (light)
1½ tbs. oyster sauce
2 tbs. good stock
1 clove garlic (chopped)
1½ tsp. sugar
2 tbs. dry sherry

Preparation
Soak dried mushrooms in water for 30 minutes. Remove stems and cut caps into halves. Wash the button mushrooms and drain.

Cooking
Heat oil in a frying pan or saucepan. When hot (a crumb will sizzle when dropped into it) add first the beans then dried mushrooms, and finally the button mushrooms (at 15 second intervals).

After 2½ minutes' frying drain away the oil (or as much as possible), and add all the sauce ingredients. Turn them with the vegetables. Reduce heat to low. Place a lid over the pan and allow contents to simmer gently for 5 minutes.

Serving
Serve hot to be consumed with rice and other dishes.

Szechuan Ma Po Tou Fu
(or Hot-Mashed Bean Curd with
Minced Meat and Peas)

(FOR 5-6 PEOPLE)

2 cakes bean curd
2 slices root ginger
2 cloves garlic
4 medium Chinese dried mushrooms
1½ tsp. salt
1 medium onion
¼-½ lb. (115-225g.) minced meat
¼ lb. (115g.) peas (fresh or frozen)
2-3 chilli peppers
4 tbs. vegetable oil
2 tbs. Tung Chai 'Winter Pickle' (optional)
1½ tbs. cornflour
5-6 tbs. good stock
2 tbs. soya sauce
1½ tbs. hoisin sauce
½ tbs. yellow bean sauce
2 spring onions

Preparation
Chop ginger, garlic, onion, chilli peppers coarsely. Soak mush-
rooms in water for ½ hour, remove stems and chop caps coarsely.
Cut bean curd into sugar-lump-size pieces. Shred spring onions.
Blend cornflour with 4 tbs. water.

Cooking
Heat oil in a large frying pan (or wok). When hot add ginger, garlic,
onion and chilli peppers. Stir them together over high heat for 1½
minutes. Add salt, minced meat and pickles. Continue to turn and
stir fry for 3-4 minutes. Add soya sauce, hoisin sauce, yellow bean
sauce, peas and stock. Stir them with the other ingredients for 2-3
minutes. Add the bean curd to stir, mix and mash with all the other
ingredients. Reduce heat and leave to cook gently together for 5
minutes. Sprinkle with spring onions and pour in the blended
cornflour. Turn and stir the contents once more and serve.

Serving
Serve in a bowl or deep-sided dish and consume with rice.

'Family-Cooked' Bean Curd with Mushrooms

(FOR 5-6 PEOPLE)

2 cakes bean curd
oil for deep frying (or semi deep frying)
6-8 medium size Chinese dried mushrooms
1-2 cloves garlic
2 slices root ginger
2 spring onions
1 tbs. Tung Chai 'Winter Pickle' (optional)
2 tbs. soya sauce
1½ tbs. hoisin sauce
1 tbs. oyster sauce
¼ pint (145 ml.) good stock
1 tsp. salt
2 tsp. sesame oil
2 tsp. chilli sauce

Preparation
Cut each cake of bean curd into 8 pieces. Deep fry or shallow fry in hot oil for 2½-3 minutes and drain. Soak dried mushrooms for ½ hour, drain and remove stems, and cut caps into quarters. Chop garlic and ginger coarsely. Cut spring onions into 1″ sections.

Cooking
Heat 3 tbs. oil in a frying pan. When hot add ginger, garlic and mushrooms. Stir fry them together for 1 minute. Add the bean curd, sprinkle with 'pickle' and salt and pour in the stock. When contents boil add all the sauces. Turn the bean curd and mushrooms over a few times in the sauce. Reduce heat and allow contents to simmer gently for 10-12 minutes. Turn the contents over a few more times and allow them to sauté in the reduced sauce for another couple of minutes. Sprinkle contents with spring onions and sesame oil.

Serving
Serve in a deep-sided dish and consume with rice.

Cold-Tossed Bean Curd

3 cakes Tou-Fu (soy bean curd)

ingredients for garnish
2 tbs. chopped Szechuan pickled green mustard
2 tbs. dried shrimps (soaked in 2 tbs. water and 2 tbs. sherry until
  softened, then chopped)
2 tbs. spring onions (chopped)

sauce ingredients
3 tbs. salad oil
1 tbs. sesame oil
2 tbs. soy sauce (light)
½ tsp. salt
2 tbs. lemon juice
1 tbs. crushed garlic
½ tbs. sugar
½ tsp. flavour powder (MSG)
¼ tsp. pepper
½ tbs. chilli sauce (Tabasco)

Preparation
Dice the Tou-Fu into sugar-lump-size cubes, put in a large bowl.
Sprinkle garnish ingredients on top of Tou-Fu then pour over the
sauce mixture (mixed together in a basin first).

Serving
Just before serving, toss and mix well; eat cold.

甜点

10. Desserts

Peking Brittle-Glazed Apple (or 'Peking Toffee Apple')

(FOR 4-5 PEOPLE)

4-5 medium apples

for batter
1 cup flour
¹/₂ cup water
1 egg
oil for deep frying

for syrup mixture
³/₄ cup sugar
1¹/₂ tbs. vegetable oil

Preparation
Peel and core apples and cut each into 4-6 pieces. Mix flour, water and egg into a well blended batter, and use this mixture to batter the apple pieces.
    Make the 'syrup' by frying the sugar and oil in a small saucepan over low heat, until the sugar dissolves, stirring all the time. Keep hot.

Cooking
Heat oil in the deep-fryer. When hot add the battered apples to deep fry for 2¹/₂-3 minutes, then remove and drain. Add them to the molten sugar to take on a coating. Quickly dip each piece in iced water to make the coating of sugar brittle. Remove and drain immediately.

Serving
Serve on an unheated serving dish. The sweet brittle coating of sugar provides a pleasing contrast to the apple underneath, especially after a long series of savoury dishes of a Chinese meal.

Peking Rough-Cut 'Ice-Mountain Fruit Salad'

(FOR 6 PEOPLE)

1 medium melon
2-3 apples
2-3 pears
2-3 peaches
some grapes
2 kiwi fruits
some strawberries (when in season)

Preparation and serving
Peel and cut all the larger fruits into pieces 3-5 times larger than usual for western fruit salads. Arrange them on top of a thick bed of chipped ice, either in a large bowl or a silver plate or tray.

Place 3-4 small saucer-size dishfuls of sugar around the fruits for the diners to use as dips. Each time the diner picks up a piece of fruit he dips it in the sugar before consuming it.

Steamed Pear in Syrup

(FOR 6 PEOPLE)

6 pears (must be firm)
4 tbs. sugar
3 tsp. syrup
6 tbs. crême de menthe

Preparation and cooking
Peel each pear except for ½" of the rim around the stem (which is left on for handling). Stand the pears in 1" of water (in a large saucepan or glass heatproof dish with lid or roasting pan with a sheet of tinfoil to cover). Sprinkle them with 2 tbs. of sugar. Bring to boil, and allow the pear to stand in the water to steam for 15 minutes. Open the top (the lid or tinfoil). Sprinkle them with remaining sugar or syrup. Raise heat to high and allow the liquid to be reduced to ¼. Pour the liqueur (use any other sweet wine or liqueur if crême de menthe is not available) over the pears and spoon the liquid in the pan over the pears half a dozen times.

Serving
Place each pear standing in a serving bowl. Pour or spoon a
quantity of syrup from pan over each pear, and serve. Can be
served hot or chilled. A good soothing dish for the throat.

'Peking Dust'

(FOR 4-5 PEOPLE)

1¼ lb. (565g.) chestnuts
1 large cup double cream
1 tsp. salt
4-5 tbs. sugar
2-3 tbs. caster sugar
1 tsp. vanilla extract

Preparation and cooking and serving
Make a criss-cross cut on each side of chestnut. Place chestnuts in
boiling water to cook for 35 minutes. Drain, cool and shell. Grind
chestnut meat and add salt and sugar. Mix until well blended. Pile
the mixture on a large serving dish and form into a mound. Whip
cream and fold in caster sugar and vanilla. Add the mixture on top
of the chestnut mound. Top it all with glazed fruits (cherries,
ginger, kumquat, etc.).
    This was a famous dessert amongst the western community in
Peking during the 1920s and 30s.

Eight Treasure Pudding

(FOR 8-10 PEOPLE)

2 cups glutinous rice
3½ cups water
5 tbs. sugar
2 tbs. vegetable oil
1 cup sweet red bean paste
*1¼ cup mixed glazed fruits (cherries, ginger, grapes, kumquats,
etc.)*
2½ tbs. lard
2 tbs. chopped almonds
2 tbs. chopped walnuts (optional)

Preparation and cooking

Wash rice and add to a saucepan with water. Bring contents to boil, and simmer them to cook gently over low heat for 12 minutes. Add oil and sugar to rice. Turn and stir until well mixed.

Rub and spread the lard evenly over the inside of a heatproof basin. Arrange and press the glazed fruit and nuts in a nice pattern at the bottom of the basin and more specially all round the sides. Add ⅓ of the rice to the bottom of the basin, being careful not to knock off any of the glazed fruit from the sides. Add a good spread of the red bean paste (about ½ of it) on top of the rice. Repeat with and add a further ⅓ of rice and remainder of bean paste. Finally cover the top with the remainder (last ⅓) of the rice.

Cover the top of the basin with tinfoil, and place it in steamer and steam for 40 minutes.

Serving

Serve by turning the pudding out on to a flat serving dish. A syrup consisting of 2 tbs. cornflour blended with 6 tbs. water and 2 tbs. sugar (with an optional 3 tbs. sweet liqueur crème de menthe or any other sweet liqueur) heated in a small saucepan until well stirred and blended may be poured over the pudding before serving.

11. Suggested Menus for Chinese Meals

When making a 'trial-run' of a Chinese meal it is best not to be over-ambitious; do not attempt to serve as many dishes as we normally do in the restaurant, where a set-meal would often run to 8 or 9 dishes. Three dishes should suffice for a simple home-cooked dinner. If the dishes are well cooked even a Chinese gourmet could find such provisioning quite adequate and satisfactory.

It is only when you are catering for more than 4-5 people, for an occasion which is something of a family party that you will need to increase the number of dishes served to 4-5. In such occasions you might prepare a soup and at least one long-cooked meat dish, which requires a minimal amount of preparation but often more than $1\frac{1}{2}$ hours to cook. With a couple of dishes taken care of in advance, by preparing and cooking them hours beforehand, one is required only to cook the quick-cooked stir-fried or quick-braised dishes just half an hour before the meal is served (hardly any of these latter dishes require as much as 10 minutes each to prepare and cook; the impression that all quick-cooked Chinese dishes consume an enormous amount of time to prepare is mistaken: the truth is that often they consume no more time to prepare than to cook which is minimal). When you are serving as many as 4 or 5 dishes with a soup the rice would then only need to be served plain (boiled or steamed), as there should be more than enough highly savoury items on the table, which all require to be cushioned and counter-balanced by a bulk food, which should be plain and unembellished. The first four of the following menus are designed for readers who want to 'break the ice' of Chinese culinary practices. These are followed by four menus where each of them is introduced by a soup, and a long-cooked meat or poultry dishs to take the pressure off the cooking and preparation, when you are perhaps entertaining in the Chinese way for the first time. The final menu provides for a good spread of dishes which could be served in the form of a 'buffet': you might be catering for 12 to 20 or more people. Chinese food is in fact eminently suitable for serving as a hot buffet.

Simple Chinese Meals of 3 dishes

(FOR 2-3 PEOPLE)

1
Long-Cooked Soya-Braised Knuckle of Pork
Vegetable Fried Rice
Cantonese Quick-Fried Beef in Oyster Sauce

2
Plain Stir-Fried Noodles with Bean-Sprouts and Mushrooms
Quick-Fried Shredded Soya Beef with Shredded Onion
Quick-Fried 'Crystal Prawns'

3
Vegetable Fried Rice
Long-Steam Lotus Leaf Wrapped Whole Fish (e.g. trout, sea-bass)
Peking Quick-Fried Diced Chicken in Soya Paste Sauce

4
Yangchow Special Fried Rice
Double-Cooked Pork
Clear Hot-Simmered Chinese Cabbage

A Peking Meal

Peking Sliced Lamb and Cucumber Soup
Sesame Prawn Toasts (prepare beforehand; deep fry at the last
moment)
Mu Shu Rou (or 'Yellow Flower Pork')
Quick-Fried Lamb with Leeks or Spring Onions in Garlic Sauce
(the last 2 dishes should be served in conjunction with rice)

A Shanghai Meal

Sweet Corn, Prawn and Crab-Meat Soup
Long-Cooked Soya-Braised Knuckle of Pork (long-cooked)
Lotus-Leaf-Wrapped and Long-Steamed Stuffed Chicken
Quick-Fried Diced Fish with Croutons, Ham and
    Straw-Mushrooms

Quick-Fried French Beans with Dried Shrimps, Garlic, Onion and
  Pickles
(the last 4 dishes should be served in conjunction with rice)

A Szechuan Meal

Hot and Sour Soup
Lotus-Leaf-Wrapped Aromatic Steamed Pork (long-cooked)
Szechuan Hot-Fried Crispy Shredded Beef
Braised Aubergine
Quick-Braised King Prawns in Shells in 'Reduced Sauce'
(the last 3 dishes should be served in conjunction with rice)

A Cantonese Meal

Wontun Soup
Cha Siu Roast Pork (roast in oven)
Cantonese Quick-Fried Beef in Oyster Sauce
Cantonese Hot-Fried Black Bean Chicken
Quick-Fried Mange Touts with Bean Sprouts
(the last 4 dishes should be served with rice)

A Chinese Buffet

When providing a good spread of dishes for a buffet for a houseful
of people — perhaps 20 of them — because of the greater number of
dishes provided than usual, the actual size of dishes to be prepared
will seldom need to be more than double the size of the recipes given
in the book. The one exception might be a couple of the bulk dishes
which everybody needs to consume in some quantity.

Five-Spice Spare Ribs
Peking Salt and Pepper Three-Spiced Choplettes
Fukien Seafood Noodles
The Hainan 'Chicken Rice'
Sesame Prawn Toasts
Cha Siu Roast Pork

Quick-Fry of 'Three Types of Cubed Meats'
Quick-Braised Courgettes in Oyster Sauce

In a buffet situation it is perhaps best not to provide a soup since it requires a bowl and tends to drip; nor to provide anything which is dripping with sauce for the same reason. All drinking should be left to short and long drinks! As far as food is concerned a good spread of Chinese dishes should provide sufficient variety to entertain all-comers. It might be best to serve the 8 dishes in two waves: the noodles with 3 supporting dishes; followed by the rice dish with the balance of dishes. For 18-20 people only the 2 bulk dishes, rice and noodles, need to be in triple portions; the rest can be just in double portions, unless of course you are providing for people with exceptional appetites, which fortunately or unfortunately are not uncommon with westerners who have taken to Chinese food!

12. Glossary

BEAN CURD A curd made from the 'milk' of ground soya beans, which have been set into cakes. Used to cook with both meat and vegetables. It is a substance distinguished by its blandness of taste, but becomes highly palatable once the flavour of sauces or other foods are added and imparted to it. It has a high protein content.

BLACK BEAN SAUCE A similar sauce to the yellow bean sauce, except, being black in colour, the beans must have been more thoroughly 'sunned' and oxidized in the process of preparation. Used in the same way as yellow bean sauce.

CHINESE SAUSAGES They are about the size of frankfurters and taste like salami sausage. They are often cooked together with other foods to provide and add a special wind-dried flavour.

FIVE SPICE POWDER A cocoa-coloured ground combination of five spices (star anise, anise pepper, fennel, cloves and cinnamon). It is fragrant and very pungent; should only be applied to food in very small quantities. Often used for roast or braised meats and poultry.

HAIR SEAWEED Marine vegetable, which is black in colour and which resembles Chinese hair. Used often for cooking in combination with other vegetables in a mixed vegetable dish.

HOISIN SAUCE Thick, dark brownish-red sauce, which is made from fermented soya beans, garlic, chilli and spices. Somewhat sweet in taste, and is frequently used as a condiment for duck, pork, spare ribs, etc, and with other meat and poultry.

LOTUS LEAF A leaf of the lotus plant's large round circular leaves, which are often used in Chinese cooking for wrapping foods for cooking (much as sheets of tinfoil are used in western kitchens).

LOTUS SEED Seed from the lotus plant, which is often used as a food ingredient in China; a white coloured seed which has an undistinguished flavour.

MSG (monosodium glutamate) Must be used sparingly. When used in quantities of less than ½ tsp, as salt and pepper are used, it can have no ill effect. When abused, and used in large quantities, it may produce what is known as 'The Chinese Restaurant Syndrome', but it will not have effects any more devastating than if salt or pepper were used in the same quantities. Therefore in cooking treat MSG as if it were salt or pepper.

OYSTER SAUCE   A south China sauce, made from oysters. It is very savoury and can be used in cooking to add flavour to both meat and vegetables.

PLUM SAUCE   A thick marmalade-like sauce, somewhat greener in colour, made from plums. Often used in conjunction with meat and poultry when crisply roasted.

RED BEAN CURD 'CHEESE'   Made from fermented bean curd; has a salty and cheesy flavour, useful for flavouring and consuming with bland food.

RED CHILLI SAUCE   A hot tasting sauce made from red chilli pepper, which can be used either as a condiment or in cooking.

SALT AND PEPPER MIX   A mixture of the two condiments, which are often supplied on the dining table for use as dips for fried food. The two ingredients are often freshly stir fried shortly together in a dry pan in order to make them into an aromatic mixture, which is when they are most effective as a condiment.

SESAME PASTE   A paste which looks and tastes like peanut butter, and in fact peanut butter can often be substituted for it.

SHARK'S FIN   Dried shark's fin, which is used by the Chinese as a food, is a delicacy; it is normally rehydrated and either cooked in a soup or long braised.

SPRING ROLL SKIN   A dough-like skin which is used for wrapping spring rolls. It is nowadays usually obtainable ready made from Chinese food stores and supermarkets.

SZECHUAN HOT JA CHAI PICKLE   A pickle made from a root vegetable, which is highly salty and peppery. Often used in adding flavour to other food materials in cooking.

TIANJIN TUNG CHAI 'WINTER PICKLE'   A light brownish pickle, often supplied in jars, which can be used to add flavour both in the cooking of meat and vegetables.

TIGER LILY STEM (also called 'Golden Needles')   Has a mouldy taste, and is used as a subsidiary ingredient mostly in vegetable cookery.

TRANSPARENT NOODLES (or 'pea starch noodles')   Usually supplied dried, like strips of cellophane; must be soaked first before being used. They are not eaten as a bulk food, as other forms of noodles, but in conjunction with other foods, whether meat or vegetables. They have a great ability to absorb quantities of stock and gravy.

WATER CHESTNUTS   Small round root-plants, not unlike radishes, but sweet in taste and less pungent to the palate. Used in Chinese cooking mostly for their crunchy texture.

WINE SEDIMENT PASTE   A paste made from the sediment at the bottom of wine jars. Very winy in taste, and often used as an ingredient for cooking, especially for seafoods, duck and game.

WONTUN SKIN   Dough skin for wrapping 'wontuns' or small 'Chinese ravioli'.

YELLOW BEAN SAUCE   A sauce or paste made from ground salted soya beans, which is extremely pungent and salty, often used for preserving food, as well as in cooking.

13.Where to Buy Ingredients

LONDON AREA

Ken Lo's Kitchen
14 Eccleston St
London SW1
01-730 4276

Loon Moon Supermarket Ltd
9A Gerrard Street
London W1V 7LJ

Loon Fung Chinese Supermarket
39 Gerrard Street
London W1

Great Wall Supermarket
31-37 Wardour Street
London W1

Chung Ying Supermarket
6 Lisle Street
London WC2

See Woo Hong
19 Lisle Street
London WC2

Walton Cheong Leen Ltd
4-10 Tower Street
Cambridge Circus
London WC2H 9NR

GREATER LONDON

Lee's Emporium
2F Dyne Road
Off Kilburn High Road
London NW6

Hoo Hing Catering Supplies
412 Green Street
Upton Park
London E13

Eastyle Ltd
11-12 Romford Shopping
Hall
Market Place
Romford
Essex

Good Companions Chinese
Supermarket
230 High Street
Croydon
Surrey

Patel Grocers
33 Fife Road
Kingston upon Thames
Surrey

Asian Food Centre
175-177 Staines Road
Hounslow
Middlesex

Bargain Grocers
61 The Broadway Market
Tooting Broadway
Tooting SW17

OUTSIDE LONDON

Quality Food Products
(Aberdeen) Ltd
Craigshaw Place
West Tullos Industrial Estate
Aberdeen

Wing Yip Supermarket
96 Coventry Street
Birmingham 5

Chung Nam Birmingham Ltd
44-46 Bromsgrove Street
Birmingham

The Delicatessen
162 Old Christchurch Road
Bournemouth
Dorset BH1 1NU

Taj Mahal Stores
216 Old Christchurch Road
Bournemouth
Dorset

Quality Foods
794-796 Leeds Road
Bradford
Yorks

Wah Hing Mini Market
148 Ashley Road
Montpelier
Bristol

Far East Emporium
62-64 Tudor Road
Cardiff

Golden Crown Oriental
Supplies
37 Crouch St
Colchester
Essex

Alma Coventry Ltd
89 Lower Precinct
Coventry

John Mann Supermarket
45 High Street
Dover
Kent

Edinburgh Chinese Company
26 Dublin Street
Edinburgh EH3 6NN

Chung Ying Supermarket
63 Cambridge Street
Glasgow C3

Chong Kee
2-6 Manthorpe Road
Grantham
Lincs

Sui Hing Supermarket
22-23 Story Street
Hull
Humberside

Hong Kong Stores
29 Lady Lane
Leeds 2

Sabat Bros
26-28 Cork Street
Leicester 4ES 5AN

Chung Wah Trading
31-32 Great George Square
Liverpool L1

Woo Sang & Company
19-21 George Street
Manchester 1ML 4HW

Wing Hing Loon Supermarket
46 Faulkner Street
Manchester M1

Wing Yip Supermarket
45 Faulkner Street
Manchester 1M1 4EE

Wing Hing Loon Supermarket
87-89 Percy Street
Newcastle Upon Tyne 1

Gill Bros & Company Ltd
(Trading as — Continental
Food Supply)
166 Kettering Road
Northampton

Wah Yam Company
77 Mansfield Road
Nottingham

Palm's Delicatessen
The Market
Oxford

Continental Fruiterers
148 Cornwall Street
Plymouth
Devon P11 1RQ

Wah Lung Supermarket
95 Mayflower Street
Plymouth
Devon

Eastern Stores
214 Kingston Road
Portsmouth

Kung Heng Co.
169 London Road
Sheffield

Yau Food Store
62 Park Road
Freemantle
Southampton

Taj Mahal
69 Derby Street
Southampton

Index